Pecuniarisation

A New Theory of Social Change in India

Pecuniarisation

A New Theory of Social Change in India

M.S. Mahendrakumar

SERIALS PUBLICATIONS
NEW DELHI

First Published - 2006

ISBN: 81-8387-039-2

Published by

SERIALS PUBLICATIONS
4830/24, Prahlad Street, Ansari Road
Darya Ganj, New Delhi-110002 (India)
Phone : 23245225. Fax : 91-11-23272135
E-mail: serials@satyam.net.in
Website: www.serialspub.com

CONTENTS

Foreword *vii*

Preface *ix*

1. Introduction 1

2. Village Ethnography 41

3. Socio-Economic Structure 72

4. Social and Cultural Interaction 103

5. Pecuniarisation—A New Theory of Social Change in India 130

6. Conclusions 189

Glossary 199

Bibliography 203

Index 215

FOREWORD

Village studies in India by social scientists resulted in the form of well-known concepts and theories and the scientists or scholars behind those concepts and theories have become famous. As far as Kerala is concerned, the village studies are a few in number and although theory building has been attempted by anthropologists and sociologists but not succeeded in their attempts. Of course, the contributions of other sister disciplines particularly social sciences and humanities cannot be negated.

Dr. M.S. Mahendrakumar has now come forward with a worthwhile publication, the impact of which will certainly be remembered for the years to come. This book is unique in two respects. Firstly, it presents first-hand and reliable village data covering all aspects of the people and their life style from various angles. Narration of qualitative data and standardisation of it through quantification help every reader to view the village life in abstract level. Secondly, this book succeeded in generalising the findings in the form of a theory called 'Pecuniarisation', which is not only applicable to Kerala villages but also village India, which is still caste based. The boundaries of traditional caste bound occupations are being dissolved, and the reasons for such dilution have been isolated and generalised in this book.

The book is written in simple language without technical jargons. The review of village studies in India,

Kerala in particular, by social scientists and Census of India in the introduction helps to get every reader the magnitude of the village life of the people living in various ecological settings conditioned by socio-economic factors. The limitation of the applicability of Sanskritization in Kerala situation has been explained explicitly in this book and therefore, the present reasoning in the form of a theory. I congratulate Dr. M.S. Mahendrakumar for presenting us a valuable theory. This book will be of much help to the social scientists involved in research on contemporary Indian society.

Palayad,
03-01-2006

Prof. (Dr.) B. Ananda Bhanu
Professor and Head
Department of Anthropology
Kannur University,
Thalassery Campus,
Palayad P.O., Kerala

PREFACE

Dynamic societies are more susceptible to change from time to time in spite of the fact that the degree of change varies from society to society. In the Indian context, the change is quite unique with its caste occupations and economic structure wherein the possibility of applicability of all the European or American social anthropological theories is rather limited. The current cultural twist in the rural areas in par with the Indian urban culture, perhaps, paved the way for a pecuniary trend among the rural mass of India. This particular trend was identified by a micro study of a Kerala village.

Generalisation of empirical data by proposing theory or concept normally receives acceptance as well as rejection by the academic community. However, the fundamental process of change of societies cannot be discarded by taking shelter or becoming the convenient user of old concepts and theories. The Indian social cultural anthropology and sociology can identify the unique Indian situation with its insightful advantages. The very uniqueness of Indian socio-economic situation is thought provoking and it ultimately led to the present theory of Pecuniarisation. Although I have proposed this theory in the beginning of 2002, but during the last three years I have been discussing and also debating with several scholars in India and abroad and that discussions virtually gave me strength to publish the theory of Pecuniarisation.

I am extremely thankful to my guru and mentor of social and cultural anthropology, Professor (Dr.) B. Ananda Bhanu, who always stimulated my analytical mind and still provokes to have a balanced thinking of social scientists. My father and mother, M.V. Sukumaran Master and C.S. Saradambal and my wife Sali V.S., are very encouraging throughout my academic pursuits and here I should also mention my sincere thanks to them. My colleagues, friends and students have been the fountain of constructive thinking and I acknowledge them all here.

Dr. M.S. Mahendrakumar
Department of Anthropology
Kannur University

1

INTRODUCTION

In rural India, extensive socio-cultural changes have occurred, which is manifest in the cultures of village communities. The way of life and the subsistence activity or the traditional caste occupation or service of a caste group was one of the decisive factors of the culture of Hindu castes. The change in the traditional caste based occupation is pervasive throughout the villages in Kerala as well as India. Many castes have abandoned their traditional caste based occupations and adopted new ones. The occupational mobility within the caste and outside can be seen in the dynamic village life. The occupational diversification sometimes provides occupational mobility within the caste or outside. In most of the cases, socio-cultural and economic factors are involved, and this involvement often ranges from the silent obligatory relationship to the explicit conflicting community level of relationship. This anxiety and predicament mostly open up new pattern of interrelationship in which people may or might have abandoned some traditional pattern of livelihood. Thus, new means of livelihood emerge and later they develop into occupational categories. Mobility within the caste occupations, and downward and upward occupational mobility on a hierarchical nature is taking place greatly.

At present, economic status of an individual is the main basis for the power and prestige in the village than the prestige attached to occupations. This shift of emphasis from the old concept of 'occupations' to a new concept provides a pattern and this process is referred to as Pecuniarisation. Downward and upward occupational mobility pertaining to a particular occupation is the fundamental character of this phenomenon and this process is taking place all over Kerala and many places in India. The theory Pecuniarisation explains the two-way process of occupational mobility where the adoption of the traditional occupation of a caste by any other caste or community either as an individual or as a group merely with an "economic motive" is defined as Pecuniarisation. Occupational diversification and occupational mobility are creating significant socio-cultural change in the village life. Castes, irrespective of their hierarchical positions, are adopting other occupations, which are capable of providing them better means of livelihood, more earnings, and higher socio-economic status. But, this mobility is neither to the direction of Brahmins nor towards dominant castes. Today, Pecuniarisation is the pattern of change taking place in village communities.

The traditional and/or caste based occupations of the castes and communities, and the changes of their occupations from caste to non-caste and traditional to non-traditional occupations are examined here. The occupations of various groups in the village were predominantly based on caste system. In the Indian context, traditionally, the members of each caste group had to perform specific functions, and that service and/or occupation was considered traditional occupation. Earlier, the villagers were confined to their own villages to satisfy most of their needs and only a few like traders, etc., were exposed to urban centres. But, now almost all people are exposed to urban centres or cities through various means.

Apart from traders, those who work in Government offices, private business establishments, hospitals, colleges, schools, and the students are regularly going to the towns, urban centres, and cities and are in regular contact with others. Only a small per cent of the villagers keep away from the adoption of different cultural traits of a heterogeneous population from the surrounding villages and urban centres.

Ishwaran (1968) opined that caste is still functional in determining an individual's occupation in most cases. But, the present study reveals that it is not a determining factor in several situations. According to Bose (1975), "changes in occupation have not become completely free and universal." Occupational mobility is pervasive and there are no restrictions as it was prevalent in the 19th century and in the early decades of 20th century. The economic system of rural India as argued by Dube (1965) is founded predominantly on the caste's functional specialisation, interdependence and occupational mobility. Caste in Indian villages to a large extent denotes occupation. Thus, occupational composition of a village is largely determined by caste composition (Madan and Dasgupta 1968). Caste is an endogamous unit, and the smallest endogamous units are the subcastes (Mayer 1960). Studies on caste and traditional occupations (Epstein 1962; Hiramani 1977) pointed out the changes of occupational patterns. The factors namely, social, cultural, religious and economic, inhibit mobility in the village communities (Ansari 1980). At present, the nature of new occupations available to the village people is crucial. The atmosphere that necessitated such occupations or formed as part of the development, and the patterns of acquiring such occupations are also important. The present study identified two major directions of occupational change such as occupational mobility outside the caste system and within the caste system. The first development is mainly due to modern education, science and technology and the occupational opportunities emerging. The second, occupational mobility within the caste system is an alternative developed due to the inadequate development of the modern system in the rural areas.

In India, a large portion of the population lives in rural areas. In Kerala, according to the Census 2001, the percentage of rural population is 74.03 and the composition of urban population is 25.97 per cent. Therefore, the knowledge about the density of the village people would be helpful to understand the majority of the population of our country and this very knowledge could be utilised for the development and welfare of the country. The research on social and cultural changes has been an indispensable area of interest for anthropologists in general and social scientists in particular throughout the world.

As far as village studies in India are concerned, the year 1871 has been marked as the beginning of the "Formulatory phase of village studies", and the publication of Sir. Henry Sumnar Maine's 'Village Communities in the East and in the West' has been considered as the pioneer study in this direction. The "Formulatory phase of village studies" continued till 1947. After India's Independence, and in the dawn of the constructive period, the publication of a long article on 'Division of labour in an Indian village' by Morris Opler and Rudra Singh in 1948, is considered as the turning point in the history of rural or village studies in India. Vidyarthi (1978) is of the opinion that, "the period of fifties in Indian anthropology may be aptly called the decade of village studies". Villages are the microcosmic units that together shape the structure of village India. According to the 1961 Census, in India there were 5,66,878 villages and according to 1991 Census the number of villages increased to 5,80,000, and a number of village studies have come out till date.

At present, there is no village in India that could be considered as a self-sufficient unit. In one way or the other, all villages are interconnected. Srinivas (1962: 78) has rightly pointed out that "the typical Indian village was not self-sufficient even before the advent of railways and buses, and it is absurd to talk of 'reviving' something that never existed".

A village study is the study of a particular unit of the whole network of villages, and the comparative study of two or more villages can be considered as the study of two or more micro units, conceived as "part-cultures". As the villages are part and parcel of the whole network of India, the villages show some general characteristics, but in contrast they show obvious differences on the eco-cultural composition. The social structure of most of the Indian villages is based on the inhabitants of the villages. Some villages are comprised of caste or castes and communities. Some villages have tribes only, or a composite of castes, tribes and religious groups. Moreover, the ecological setting of the villages also varies. The studies on the villages vary from socio-cultural, socio-economic, historical, geographical, and physical aspects to the diverse eco-systems. Anthropologists, sociologists, economists, historians and geographers, have conducted extensive studies of various villages.

Indian Village Studies

On the basis of the coverage, the village studies can be broadly categorised into two viz., (i) the studies providing stationary or static aspects and (ii) the studies focusing change. While some studies were synchronic in nature, a few of them had been essentially diachronic. Many village studies conducted in India were on the heterogeneous population. Vidyarthi (1978) points out that the number of publications on caste system is well over six thousand. Some of the earlier studies can be categorised as village or rural studies as well as caste studies. The emphasis of some studies was primarily on the caste and its hierarchies.

The studies of Wiser (1936), Ghurye (1942), Srinivas (1942), and Hutton (1946) were some of the significant attempts of the constructive period of the village studies. Morris Opler's 'Village Life in North India' (1951), Srinivas's 'Caste in Modern India and Other Essays' (1962), Oscar Lewis's 'Group Dynamics in a North Indian Village' (1954), Majumdar's 'Caste and Communication in an Indian Village' (1958), etc., are some of the important studies conducted during the dawn of the analytical period. Of these, the works of Wiser (1936), Srinivas (1942), Opler (1951), Lewis (1954), and Majumdar (1958) analyse the caste and its dynamics within the villages of India, and hence they can be referred to as village studies as well as caste studies.

Mysore Narasimhachar Srinivas, who was one of the eminent social anthropologists of India, made a number of village studies from various dimensions. His essays and works, namely, 'Religion and Society among the Coorgs of South India' (1952), 'India's Village' (1955), 'The Social System of Mysore Village' (1955), 'The Dominant Caste in Rampura' (1959), 'Caste in Modern India and Other Essays' (1962), Social Change in Modern India' (1972), and 'The Remembered Village' (1976) paved the way for a number of social theories in the field of socio-cultural anthropology in India. The concept, "Sanskritization", postulated by Srinivas through his second doctoral thesis: 'Religion and Society among the Coorgs of South India', has become an instrument for locating the process, through which the lower castes or tribes try to model their behaviour along the styles of life of the upper varnas of the Hindu society.

In the first essay of his book 'Caste in Modern India and Other Essays' (1962) captioned 'Caste in Modern

India', Srinivas has attempted to highlight the part played by caste in the democratic processes of modern India, and in administration and education. Another essay, 'The industrialisation and urbanisation of rural areas', discusses the changes in villages in the pre-British India and also Independent India. Srinivas has examined the changes that have occurred in a few villages, namely, Manhalli, Namhalli, Rampura, and Kumbapetti. Originally, Kathleen Gough (1951-52), Scarlett Trent (1955), and Alan R. Beals (1960), conducted studies on the villages of Kumbapetti, Manhalli, and Namhalli respectively. Srinivas studied the village of Rampura, in Mysore district, in 1948 and again in 1952. Srinivas also made a short note on the changes of these villages, in a subsequent essay. Further, 'A Note on Sanskritization and Westernization' gives the profile of two social processes in modern India and it is not possible to understand one without reference to the other. When there is Sanskritization, mobility may be said to occur within the framework of caste, whereas Westernisation implies mobility outside the framework of caste. For Srinivas, the concept Sanskritization was found useful in the analysis of the social and religious life of the Coorgs of South India. It was in 1952 that Srinivas used the term, 'Sanskritization' to describe the process of cultural mobility in the traditional social structure for the first time in his book 'Religion and Society among the Coorgs of South India'. "The usefulness of Sanskritization as a tool in the analysis of Indian society is greatly limited by the complexity of the concept as well as its looseness" (Srinivas, 1962: 44). In his study on the Coorgs in Mysore he found that the lower castes, with a view to raising their position in the caste hierarchy, adopted some customs of the Brahmins and gave up some of their own, which were considered to be impure by the higher castes. To denote this process of mobility, Srinivas first used the term

Brahminization, which was later replaced by the term Sanskritization. "Sanskritization is a much broader concept than Brahminization"(Srinivas, 1962). He redefined it as: "Sanskritization is the process by which a "low" Hindu caste, or tribal or other group, changes its customs, ritual, ideology and way of life in the direction of a high, and frequently of a "twice born" caste. Generally such changes are followed by a claim to a higher position in the caste hierarchy than that traditionally conceded to the claimant caste by the local community" (Srinivas, 1972: 6). According to Srinivas, Sanskritization seems to have occurred throughout Indian history and still continues to occur. Westernisation, on the other hand, refers to changes introduced into Indian societies during British rule and which continue, in some cases with added momentum, in independent India. The complex and intricate interrelation between Sanskritization and Westernization, on a short-term as well as long-term basis, offers a fertile field for analysis and speculation.

Ishwaran's (1968) book 'Shivpur: A South Indian Village', is based on an empirical study conducted in the Shivpur village situated between the two cities of Hubli and Dharwar in the erstwhile Mysore state. The significance of this study is that it checks the applicability of Srinivas's concepts, Sanskritization and Westernization. Ishwaran logically criticises those concepts and points out that, "Srinivas considers 'Sanskritization' as the process whereby mobility takes place within the framework of caste. He maintains that dominant castes accelerate or retard these processes by a dominant caste, he means one that is numerically superior, ritually superior, and controls the economy of the village. It is our [Ishwaran, et al.] thesis that the hypothesised relationship between supposed caste dominants and some process like Sanskritization is simply inapplicable to Shivpur. One caste, ... the Lingayat, which has a majority, is ritually superior to the others, and is in relative control of farming, the basis of the village economy. But it cannot claim ascendancy over the other castes. The 'dominant' caste exercises no power over other castes, which are not prescribed by the Hindu tradition, and which it would not exercise by that tradition even where it is not 'dominant'. Thus it is not in a position to speed up or retard some mythical 'Sanskritization' process. Shivpur is becoming neither 'sanskritized' nor 'westernised', but is adapting its traditional order to meet the exigencies of modern living without abandoning or changing its traditional character in any essential respect" (Ishwaran, 1968: 30-31). In addition to this Ishwaran argues that the change and continuity cannot be explained by the concepts, Sanskritization and Westernization, as it would be "oversimplifications" and "unilateral determinism of an idealistic kind". He is of the opinion that there are six factors-the street, lineage, sub-caste, caste, region and village-that draw people closer, and five factors that draw apart–land, the Panchayat, the co-operative societies, village feuds and membership of faction groups. The key-institution of caste tends to be more open in formal, political and economic activities but closed in other areas of life.

About the functional role of the castes, he (Ishwaran: ibid.) delineates that, "Caste is still functional in determining an individual's occupation in most cases. Occupational and social mobility is next to impossible. Surplus labour in any occupation goes to neighbouring villages, where it occupies its traditional place. A goldsmith can never become a carpenter; a carpenter can never become a barber. Endogamy and traditional relations of personal dependence between persons, coupled with personal pride, considerations of honour, and the social pressure of ridicule, help to maintain the economic closeness of caste".

Through the first few chapters Ishwaran describes that the village Shivpur is dominated by a traditional economy in spite of its proximity to the nearby urban centres and its access to means of communication, etc. In the village, there are 13 castes and 40 sub-castes. Each person is born into a lineage, which is a part of a sub-caste, which in turn is part of a caste. In the last few chapters, he points out the change and continuity of the social structure of Shivpur. The occupational structure, and the economic system in general are becoming more open, and on the other hand, caste and kinship are actually becoming more closed. In general, Ishwaran's monograph on the problems of a single village is a comprehensive account.

A monograph, 'Indian Village', published by Dube (1955), is based on a fieldwork in a village Shamirpet in Andhra Pradesh, and it includes a detailed picture of the functioning of village institutions. Dube underscores the fact that the economic system of rural India is founded predominantly on the caste's functional specialisation, interdependence and occupational mobility. The village Shamirpet, located about 25 miles from Hyderabad, has a heterogeneous population comprising of Muslims and 19 different Hindu castes.

Another significant work of Dube (1958) (reviewed in Chauhan, 1974: 101), 'India's Changing Villages', discusses the situation in two nearby villages in Saharanpur district of U.P. According to Chauhan, "the study is significant for being the first in studying the effects of community development in India. It remains essentially a qualitative study and does not try to explain differences".

Lewis (1958) has made a significant village study entitled 'Village life in Northern India'. It was conducted in a Delhi village and he is of the opinion that "although there is a great deal of literature about the caste system of India, very little attention has been paid to its economic aspects. Most books and articles on caste have concerned themselves with the problems of its historical origin and development, with the rules and sanctions governing endogamy, food taboos, ritual purity, caste ranking, and the more dramatic injustices or untouchability. It is common in works about caste for the author to list the castes of a particular region with some account of the traditional occupation of each... but it is a curious fact that the author generally avoids what might logically seem to be a next step–an analysis of how these groups interact with one another in the production and exchange of goods and services" (1958: 55). Lewis (ibid.) attempts to analyse the functioning of the Jajmani system in Rampur village. The caste groups of Rampur have traditionally been related to one another through mutual obligations of the Jajmani system. It is a characteristic of this system to operate without much exchange of money. The Jajman compensates his Kamins for their work through payments in cash or grain, made throughout the year on a daily, monthly or biyearly basis. Kamins may also receive benefits such as free food, clothing, and residence site, the use of certain tools and raw materials, etc. A major function of the Jajmani system is to ensure a stable labour supply for the dominant agricultural caste in a particular region by limiting the mobility of the lower castes, especially those who assist in agricultural work. Lewis observed the changes in this system due to modern improvements, technological changes, India's five-year plans, and the influence of reformist movements and political ideologies. The study reveals that the Camars have stopped fulfilling some of their Jajmani obligations towards the Jats who have reciprocated in turn. There are also indications of tension between the Jats and the Bhanis, although the latter continue to serve their Jajmans. The Brahmans have lost their priestly functions. The Dhobis, who formerly depended completely upon their local Jajmans, now have customers in Delhi as well. The Khatis and the Lohars are abandoning their traditional trades. The Nais have lost their roles as marriage go-betweens as well as some of their job opportunities as barbers. Some of their former Jajmans shave themselves; their wives shampoo their own hair. In essence, most of the lower-caste villagers and many of the Jats are in debt. Some of them have been forced to change their occupations and have gone to Delhi to look for work. Technological changes and the increasing land fragmentation have reduced the need for help in agriculture among the Jat families. Meanwhile, the Arya Samaj and some political parties have preached effectually, against caste restrictions. All these factors have led to a loosening of jajmani ties and obligations. The study also points out that despite the weakening of the Jajmani system and the inroads of a money economy in Rampur, the social aspects of the caste system have changed very little. Patterns of hierarchy and social distance persist, and the caste-psychology still permeates interpersonal relationships. The study concludes saying that the decline of the Jajmani system will not necessarily be followed by an automatic or speedy disintegration of the caste. It may rather continue to take on new functions and manifestations.

The study, 'Caste and Kinship in Central India: A Village and its Region' (Mayer 1960) describes the caste system as it operates in a multi-caste village and its surroundings. It also deals with the internal and external relations of village and local caste groups. This book is based on his fieldwork at Ramkheri located at a distance of seven miles from a small town called Dewas on the plateau of Malwa village and 30 miles from Ujjain. In 1952, Ramkheri was a village having 912 persons with 27 Hindu castes and Muslim castes. Mayer used the term 'Muslim caste' for these Muslim groups, who are endogamous, and have many customs foreign to Islam though consistent with their caste customs before conversion. The people of these castes are conscious of this, and distinguish themselves and other similar Muslim castes (Mewati, Naitu, etc.) from those they call 'Musulman' (ibid. 34-35). He delineates the limits of the locally effective caste and subcaste groups and the mechanisms controlling their members in relation to each other and with people of other castes. Mayer has identified three levels of membership in a caste. They are, first, the kindred of co-operation, which is the lowest one of an effective local subcaste population; second, the kindred of recognition, is the population around the kindred of co-operation, and within which marriages are made and/or kin links can be traced through mutual kin. The kindred of recognition are an endogamous one. Third, beyond these two kindreds there are people, who are recognised as members of a subcaste, which is endogamous, named, and separated from other subcastes. Further, Mayer integrates these three levels with caste and many subcastes, which make up a caste. Caste is an endogamous unit and the smallest endogamous units are the subcastes. On the whole, caste membership is significant for relations with other castes, and subcaste membership for activities within the caste. In turn, these activities are in fact based on the decisions of a local kindred. Again, every man is a member of three bodies–the kindred, the subcaste and the caste. Mayer, further, describes how this membership is acquired. Part II of that book focuses on the village and the caste. It includes an analysis of inter-caste relations, and the way these are related to the 'unity' of the single village. Part III deals with the divisions within the caste – subcaste, and the clan, the lineage, etc., and their loci in the village and region. Chapter on 'caste and ritual status' describes the structure of the commensal hierarchy of the village. It examines the ritual status of caste on the basis of commensal hierarchy. The commensal hierarchy is based on the theory that each caste has a certain quality or ritual purity that is lessened, or polluted, by certain commensal contacts with castes having an inferior quality. Commensal contacts include the cooking of food and its consumption. A superior caste will not eat from the hands of a caste that it regards as inferior, nor will its members sit next to the inferior people in the same unbroken line while eating. Similar rules of exclusion are observed in drinking and smoking. He has illustrated the commensal relations of twenty-five Hindu and two Muslim castes in Ramkheri.

The chapter, 'Economic aspects of caste', analyses the economic pattern in the village Ramkheri. The description and analysis of the economic aspects of caste cover mainly the traditional bases of occupation, the hierarchy of occupations, caste, occupation, etc. Mayer is of the opinion that the traditional occupation of a caste and its commensal position are closely related. He exemplifies that a caste having a polluting occupation could not have a high commensal status. When such a caste wishes to change their status, they first try to disassociate themselves from their traditional occupation. Only when this has been done, the caste members claim a higher commensal rank, and partly back up the demand with evidence of their new occupational status. In essence, Mayer's main aim was to inquire into the nature of the caste and subcaste. He concludes that, caste defines a village group and it is based on traditional occupation, commensal regulations and a particular status and mode of behaviour in the village. Mayer's study is of great importance as it highlights the major elements like caste, kinship, social structure, etc., within a village and their nexus and extensions in the surrounding regions. The analysis of these elements and the cultural milieu rightly points out the necessity of the coverage of the objectives of a comprehensive village study. Mayer (1960; 1986 rpt.: 24) has rightly pointed out that, "it would be impossible to discuss any major aspect of the villager's life without mentioning his caste. The manner of the rites he performs, often his occupation, the kind of social and economic relations he has with his fellow-residents, all vary with caste membership".

In 1962, Epstein, a British Anthropologist, published a book entitled 'Economic Development and Social Change in South India', based on two years fieldwork in 1954 -'55, in two villages: a wet village, Wangala and a dry village, Danela, in the same region in Mysore. In this full-length village study, she makes an attempt to bring out the impact of irrigation on the economic and social organisation of the village within a regional economy. She concludes that the economic change alters the socio-cultural organisation. In 1963, Ghurye published a book, 'The Anatomy of a rural-urban community'. It surveyed 117 villages including eight agricultural towns, some big and small villages in the Haweli taluk in Maharashtra.

Madan and Dasgupta (1968) made a comparative study of two villages in Uttar Pradesh. This monograph covers mainly the land and agriculture, caste structure, leadership structure, etc., in two villages, namely, Ladpur and Pampur. Occupational compositions of the two villages also have been examined in this study. Caste in Indian villages also to a large extent denotes occupation. Thus, occupational composition of a village is largely determined by caste composition. This study attempts to compare the caste structure of the two villages, which are at different levels of agricultural practice and development. It tried to relate the former to the latter. The two villages also varied in three important components of its social structure such as caste, leadership and opinion. The study concludes by projecting the significance of the analysis of the interrelated components of social system and its unique structure.

Mann (1972) delineated the social stratification in Ladakhi villages and analysed the social interaction of the people of the village. All the four villages studied are predominantly Buddhist, having Ladakhi (Bhautta) as the dominant group. The Gara, Mon and Beda are the other groups. He is of the opinion that, like the Hindu society of village India, the stratification is also a feature of Ladakhi Buddhist society. All these social groups in Ladakhi villages have specific occupations. Like the castes, these groups have a set of norms of behaviour. These rules regulate the intra and inter-group relations in various ways of life. In the light of features like specific name, specific occupation, fixed position in social hierarchy and endogamy, as applicable to Ladakhi, Gara, Mon and Beda, it can be inferred that they are heading to the formation of a caste-like society. Further, this study mentions that under the changing conditions, economic prosperity, the educational standard and superior position in service do not help to elevate the social position of a person. His basic position continues to be recognised with his affiliation to a specific group.

Bose (1975) examines the changes in the ancient way of life in a Bengal village, Jajigram, comprising twenty-eight castes. The study explains the traditional occupations and the changes. Bose shows that even when people do not leave their ancient homes and retain territorial or geographical separateness to an appreciable extent, changes in occupation may be proportionately more extensive than the physical movements involved. The study also analysed some of the factors of occupational change. The study has pointed out that, when it became impossible to earn one's living in Bengal by means of the traditional hereditary occupations, a more or less urbanised middle class began to emerge from among all

Hindu castes as well as Muslims, and it is one of the roots which held caste firmly. It is also pointed out that changes in occupation have not become completely free and universal.

'Changing traditions of a low caste' is a paper by Cohn (1975 rpt.), who conducted a fieldwork in 1952–1953 among the Camars of Uttar Pradesh. The Camars are a widespread and numerically important population of North India. Their traditional occupation is skinning, tanning, and working in leather; but only a small number of this extensive caste derives its income from the traditional occupation, and the great majority make their living as agricultural labourers and, increasingly in the twentieth century, as urban labourers. The study remarks that literacy has enabled the Camars to relate to aspects of the Hindu Great Tradition through reading stories available in vernacular books. Urban employment has enabled Camars to participate in rituals, derived from the Hindu Great Tradition, at low caste temples in the Cities. Simultaneously there continues an earlier movement, the Siva Narayan sect, whose goal was Sanskritization. These are the four important aspects aiming at raising the Camars' low social status. In essence, the paper presents a number of new social and economic situations, which affect the traditions of a group of Camars in an Uttar Pradesh village.

Singer (1975 rpt.) has used a comparative analysis of cultural performances as a method for studying the structure and changes of a cultural tradition, and particularly of the interactions of the Great and Little tradition in his paper, 'The Great Tradition in metropolitan centre: Madras'. According to him, through an analysis and comparison of cultural performances and their constitutions, it is possible to construct the structure and organisation of particular kinds of performances. By tracing the linkages among these structures and organisations, it is possible to arrive at the more comprehensive and abstract constructs of social structure, value system, and a Great tradition. The study argues that the folk performances are close to the little tradition and are performed generally by members of the non-Brahmin community, whereas the sacred sphere is closely associated with Brahmins and the Great tradition. The effect of urbanisation also has been analysed in this study. Changes from cultural media to mass media and from sacred centres and occasions of performance to cultural centres and secular attitudes are also delineated.

The book entitled 'Social organisation of Amnari: A village study in Chotanagpur' is written by Varma (1977), based on a comprehensive fieldwork made in 1964 and 1968 in the Amnari village, which is also located in the tribal belt of Chotanagpur. The population of the village consists mainly of Hindus. There are 16 castes, two tribal communities such as the Santhal and Birhor, and the Muslims. Varma has examined the inter-relationship of these tribes and Muslims with the Hindus in Amnari to show the integration of a heterogeneous village in Bihar. The emphasis in this study is on the inter-caste and inter-group interaction, which brings about the unity and solidarity of the village community.

Hiramani (1977) has conducted a study in two villages namely, Kolghar and Golatgaon. Both these villages have heterogeneous population consisting of different castes and communities. A broad perspective of the villages provides occupational information too. The study analyses the nature of population engaged in their traditional non-traditional occupations as the principal source of livelihood. The families of the Kolghar village have mostly given up their traditional occupations, whereas, in the Golatgaon village, most of the people continue their traditional occupations and the number of families following traditional occupations is more than those who follow non-traditional occupations.

The study has also analysed the occupational mobility of various generations of different castes and religious groups (Buddhists and Muslims).

Kundu, (1978) has conducted a study on the Landowner-tenant relationship in Vinzar, a dispersed village situated in Haveli taluk of Poona district in Maharashtra. Twenty-one caste groups live in this village but only fourteen castes own cultivable land. According to the author, landowner-tenant relationship was more conspicuous during the time of Jagirdari and Zamindari systems. Now-a-days, only sharecropping gives the form of landowner-tenant relationship, and it has stemmed from the abolition of Jagirdari and Zamindari systems. Gupta (1978) also made a study on the occupational mobility of some castes in Ponnampet, a Coorg village. The study has made comparisons of the occupations of three generations of twelve caste groups and a community. By taking up various occupations and business, they have changed their mode of livelihood. The study reveals that there has been a complete change from traditional to some other occupations.

Rizvi (1979) made a comparative study of the Bodhs of Spiti and the Muslims of Kargil. The study attempts to describe the social stratification in Spiti. It is similar to tho caste model in comparison to the Muslims of Kargil, but, according to the author, in other places in India the Muslims show clear signs of caste system. Kameswara Rao (1979) argues in his paper, 'Saga of development in Telengana village', that the outlook and attitude of villagers towards a particular programme is not vague but pragmatic. A descriptive account on the problems involved in the rural reconstruction and development programmes covers the different reactions of various sects in a multicaste village. They show greater concern for the bare necessities of life, and are not interested in goals beyond their span of attainment.

Misra (1979) made a study on the actual spatial, social and economic distances that prevail between the Harijans, the lowest among the peasantry, and the rest of the rural society in the Palayasivaram village in Walayabad taluk, Chingleput district, in Tamil Nadu. The study describes the inter-caste interactions of the earlier time and the changes, which have appeared in the present day. Earlier, within the village, each caste group had a street to live in, and there was hardly any case of encroachment of one another among the various castes. But some castes like Mudaliars and Naickens are now living together in some streets, which are newly occupied by them due to expansion of their families. It is also pointed out that the site of the houses of the members of various castes is again in proportion to the comparative social distances between them. The study observes the socio-economic changes too among the Weaker Sections. The author concludes that, "the economic disparity coupled with social norms have more or less maintained the traditional pattern of social relations not withstanding some improvements devised to meet the new situations" (Misra 1979).

Madan (1979) in his book, 'India's Social Transformation Vol. I: Problems of the Economic Development', has included a chapter on 'Caste and Occupational Mobility'. It is a study based on his fieldwork in two villages in Lucknow district in Uttar Predesh, which delineates various occupations of the people of these villages. The study concludes that the upper castes like the Brahmins and the Thakurs still consider manual work and business as degrading occupations. Whereas, among the intermediate castes, there are ample opportunities for mobility, and there is no caste barrier whatsoever to follow any occupation in the present age. However, those intermediate castes, which think that their social status is equal to that of the Thakurs and the Brahmins, do not engage in trade or manual labour. Even among the rest of the group there are few families engaged in business (exception being the Telis and Kurmis) this is the basis of industrial development. The members of the lower castes work as manual workers and do menial jobs. Madan (ibid: 219) argues that "studying the situation as a whole we may say that the upper castes such as Brahmins and Kshatriyas and dominating castes among the intermediate, i.e., Ahirs who have enough education and resources, have no aptitude for business or manual work, which is a serious hindrance to industrial development in this region". Madan also studied the problems of village leadership and community development, health and family planning programme in rural India and non-formal education programmes in Uttar Pradesh. All these four chapters are based on empirical studies, and published in the second part of his book. The first part of the book deals with the objectives of economic development in India, the problems of industrialisation, urbanisation, rural-urban integration and regional development, changes in social organisation, and the need for planned change.

Ansari (1980) in his book on 'The Changing Village India' opines that the National Extension Service Programme carried out under the Community Development Programme has been very successful in making significant impact of universal character on the total rural traditional structure. Nevertheless, he has also pointed out some of the drawbacks in the new system. The author has attempted to analyse the role of the Community Development and National Extension Programme and their impact on the social and economic life of people of the Maner Community Development Block in the Patna district in Bihar. It has analysed the factors working as agents of promotion, viz., social traditions and socio-economic change, bureaucracy and progressive development, role of modern programmes and traditional social values, secularisation of attitude and adoption of innovations, execution of progressive development programmes, and role of extension functionaries in reconstruction. The study also presents the extent of movement of rural manpower to urban-industrial centres in the country, and Ansari is of the opinion that the nature of the occupational mobility is unplanned, unstable and highly flexible. The study reveals the changing pattern of occupations and occupational mobility. It has also highlighted the barriers, namely, social, cultural, religious and economic, that inhibit mobility in the village communities.

Gupta (1981) made a study on the village organisation and inter-village solidarity among the Purum Chote of Manipur. He assesses the impact of Christianity and other current forces in these aspects. The Purum Chote is interspersed in the south-eastern part of Manipur in the district of Tengnoupal.

Some scholars like economists, historians, anthropologists, geographers, etc., from various institutions of Japan, the University of Madras, and the Madurai-Kamaraj University, have collaborated in a research project organised by the Institute for the Study of Languages and Cultures of Asia and Africa, in Tokyo; and conducted a series of socio-cultural studies in some villages in Tamil Nadu. The reports of these studies were published during 1981, '82, '83, and 1984, under the title 'Studies in Socio-Cultural Change in Rural Villages in Tiruchirapalli District, Tamil Nadu, India: No. 1 to 5'. In connection with the above research project, Subbiah (1981), Department of Geography in the University of Madras, has written a paper entitled 'Rural Base in a South Indian Village: A Study into its Structural and Spatial Patterns in Mahizambadi village of Tamil Nadu', in the 'Studies in Socio-Cultural Change in Rural Villages in Tiruchirapalli District, Tamil Nadu, India; (No–4). Subbiah's study concludes that for planning an efficient utilisation of basic resources and the process behind the rural scene has to be thoroughly probed. Another paper presented in the same interim report is that of Tsukasa Mizhshima and Tsuyoshi Nara (1981), entitled 'Social Change in a Dry Village in South India: An Interim Report'.

Nakamura (1982) from the Institute of Developing Economies in Japan, has conducted fieldwork and socio-economic survey in a village at the Thuraiyur taluk of Tiruchirapalli district of Tamil Nadu, during 1979 –1980 and published an interim report entitled 'Disintegration and Reintegration of a Rural Society in the Process of Economic Development, A Second Survey of a Tank-based village in Tamil Nadu'. Another Japanese scholar, Karashima (1983), Professor of South Asian History, University of Tokyo, has edited a book on the historical background of the village and its socio-cultural change, and this book is entitled as 'Socio-Cultural Change in Villages in Tiruchirapalli District, Tamil Nadu, India; Part One, Pre-Modern Period'.

Komoguchi (1984), a Geographer of the Komazawa University in Japan, has conducted a study on 'A South Indian Village: Its Agriculture and Community". This study was based on the caste, household, and individual levels under a specifically classified size of landholdings. Each caste group has been regarded as an analytical unit of the study. The trend of inter-caste relationship in the village has also been studied. The study concludes that, by considering the present trend of population growth, a way to secure stable life in future does not seem to be found in any agricultural means for the coming generation. The fundamental solution to various problems now confronting the villages in South India can be found in developing non-agricultural industry to absorb the surplus population from the village concerned.

Chakraborti (1983) has made some observations on the management of land and labour in a West Bengal village, in Burdwan district, which has experienced massive I.A.D.P. programmes since 1962. The study points out the pattern of landholdings by various castes and communities in the village. It analyses the groups of people who are involved in the management of land and organisation of production. According to the pattern of land holding, there are broadly two groups of people; the first group is of the Hindu upper castes and the Muslim who together possess 96.91 per cent of the total land. The second group comprises the Hindu lower castes and the Santal tribe. The study has also pointed out some instances of occupational mobility, migration of labourers, etc. The study describes the pattern of management of land and labour with regard to the socio-economic context.

Sarkar (1984) in his study, 'Occupational mobility among the artisan groups of Mysore City', examines the occupational mobility among the 'caste-bound' as well as 'caste-free' artisans. When there are several instances of occupational mobility, particularly appearing during the current generation, the apparently 'caste-free' occupations are also subjected to a definite pattern and assuming the characteristics of 'caste-bound' occupations. In the cases of shift from 'caste-bound' occupations to 'caste-free' ones, however, people were keen to select those that were considered socio-ritually relatively superior.

A study on 'Changing agrarian relations and the ethnic process in a cluster of villages around the market town of Boinchee in Hooghly district of West Bengal' is a significant village study by Roy Burman (1984). The study covers seven villages namely, Piragram, Jamna, Insura, Bhoupur, Chetna, Sargaria and Bhuimohan. The study explains the ramification of a few important aspects such as the enactment of the Land Reform Act and Land Acquisition Act, in 1950s. The Land Reform Act became a signal for the eviction of a large number of sharecroppers. Similarly, the Land Acquisition Act caused the creation of benami transfers. The relationship between landowners and agricultural labourers and sharecroppers became tense. The proliferation of quasi-political and quasi-religious gurus, the development activities under the aegis of the National Extension Service Programme, Krishak Samities, the government led by the leftist parties in 1967,etc., were some of the major elements involved in the changing agrarian relations. The study rightly highlights the correlations between ethnic identity and role differentiation in the management of land and agricultural production.

Morab, et al. (1985) attempt to highlight the agrarian situation in Hirearakere, a village in Chitradurga district of Karnataka state. The study focuses on the agrarian situation among the small and medium farmers belonging to different caste groups. It is remarked that a high percentage of medium and small farmers continue capitalised mode of agricultural production based on profit oriented calculation. The authors argue that the farmers carry a great amount of social status attached to agriculture.

Ekka (1985) has studied the caste hierarchy and inter-ethnic relationship in a village of Surguja district in Madhya Predesh. The village community of Sardi is composed of sixteen different ethnic groups comprising castes, tribes and the Muslims. It reveals the caste hierarchy, on the basis of the commensal relationship and the traditional occupation of the castes and tribes. The inclusion of tribes and Muslim in the "caste hierarchy" was justified by Dube (1955:7), on the ground that "the hierarchical organisation of castes within the community is so fixed in the structural pattern of rural India that the tribal as well as non-Hindu (such as Muslim and Christian) segments of the population come to be regarded as other castes in the village" (quoted in Ekka, 1985; 177). The paper traces the extant of some of the elements of caste system, namely, birth determines one's caste, traditional occupation with its relative ritual purity and pollution, food, etc., and in the Sardi village, the caste hierarchy is based on these things to a large extent. Inter-ethnic relationships were also described in the study.

Danda's (1986) paper, 'Development perspectives and the rural poor', is based on a study in five villages in five different States, namely, West Bengal, Tripura, Assam, Orissa and Bihar. The study remarks that the Weaker Sections could be identified in terms of caste and community. It covers various aspects such as economic, political, socio-ritual, etc. The case studies indicate that due to non-egalitarian flow of developmental efforts the conditions of the poor are becoming increasingly acute. It also depicts a picture of rural weakness in the context of apparently isolated village communities. The study has essentially touched the changing and diversifying occupational scene of the villages. It also emphasises that for depicting the Indian social situation, reference to the varna-jati model has been found inevitable. It concludes that all apparent developmental measures introduced to bring about change seem to contribute towards mere maintenance of the existing structure.

Danda (1986) has made a study on the forms and nature of stratification in Basudha, a village in West Bengal. It has tried to classify the Hindu castes of the village into three segments, namely, upper, middle, and lower. The upper segment is occupied by the Brahmin and Kayastha. The middle segment is occupied by four castes who have rather a marginal position in the hierarchy. The lower segment is formed by eight groups. Ranking of castes and communities on the basis of ritual, economic and socio-political factors has also been attempted. In general, stratification is conceived as a graded system of individual status within a group, community, or organisation, or as a formation of social classes, castes, strata or levels into a hierarchy of prestige. According to Danda, the data from this village clearly demonstrate that if hierarchy and relative accessibility to resources and privileges are taken as indices of stratification, distinctions between age-grades and sexes can perhaps be explained in terms of manifestation of the system of stratification as well. It also mentions that the assignment of jobs in this village is regulated through a fairly intricate as well as rigid system of caste, control over economic resources, age, sex, etc.

Dutta (1987) has explained the emerging relations of production in rural India. He has examined the problem in three contiguous villages, namely, Manikpur, Sujanpur, and Shankarpur, in Rohtas district in Bihar. The study analyses the agrarian structure on the basis of occupations. It infers that the majority of rich peasants are non-cultivating owners when compared to other classes of peasants. Therefore, they depend upon 'purchase of labour power' of others for cultivation. Among the middle group of peasants, the service holders are more. Further, the labourers are mainly from the poor and landless peasants. Now the poor peasants have started trading activities and do not always live by selling their labour. But the landless-cum-poor peasants concentrate more in the working class and sell their labour to the rich for survival and become more and more dependent on the rich peasants. The study describes the important classes of peasantry, and in general, it has covered the agrarian structure of Bihar village.

Mukhopadhyay (1989) has made a study of a Karnataka village on the democratisation of village panchayat. It attempts to assess the differential influence of three factors, namely caste, politics, and economy in the formation and functioning of the village level panchayat. It also infers that the extent of politics and economy in reducing the caste factor from the democratisation process of the village panchayat in Hampapura village in Krishnarajanagar taluk in Mysore district, Karnataka. The study observes that since 1960 there has been no qualitative change in the situation. The primary functioning of the statutory panchayat, as it was structured and functioning, is on the basis of economic factors and ethnic affiliation, and the factor of political power comes only to a secondary position. Politics and economy did not help considerably to replace the caste factor to bring about a 'mature democratic political system' at the village level panchayat.

Sivaram (1990) has made a sociological study entitled 'social mobility'. The study examined the occupational mobility patterns and socio-economic conditions among the five backward castes namely, Chakali (washerman), Devanga (silk and yarn weaver), Kummari (potter), Mangali (barber), and Padmasala (only yarn weaver), in Proddatur town of Cuddapah district, in Andhra Predesh. The data was collected from 600 respondents (male Head of the families only) taking 120 respondants from each caste. The study reveals that there is no evidence of occupational rigidity. It means that although occupations are strictly caste bound, it is possible even for the lower caste people to change their occupations and achieve upward mobility. Immigration has also played a significant role in the occupational mobility. Education is also a factor for occupational mobility and the extent of literacy and educational attainment has continued to rise from one generation to another. The study also indicates that the caste system as a determinant in occupational choice is still a dynamic force; and that there are castes, which are occupationally oriented in the sense that a few select backward castes are following their occupations. In essence, it deals with the nature of occupational mobility, causes for occupational mobility, the family, marriage among the castes and also their attitude towards their traditional and non-traditional occupations. The universe of the study was an urban area.

A study on the 'agro-economic organisation among the Jats', the main land holding group, in a South Rajastan village, was done by Mandal and Bhakrabarth (1991). The study was conducted in Mavli village, comprising more than 30 endogamous castes and communities, in the Udaipur district. The economic life of the Jats of Mavli greatly depends on land and agriculture. A few of them are engaged in other occupations like services, trade, etc., but they never give up cultivation and they, in general, prefer their traditional technology rather than modern technology of production in agriculture. The Jats call themselves Kastekar meaning cultivator or the tiller of the soil. They put their own labour in cultivation. Family labour is considered the most important, since both male and female participate in agriculture. But for a big farmer, family labour always falls insufficient than required; therefore, they have to depend on hired labourers to a great extent. Farmer-labourer relationship is cordial as the farmers and the labourers work together in the field. It is also pointed out that the farmers of Mavli feel that if proper irrigation facility is made available in the area, their lands will give higher yields, and it is possible only if the government takes the initiative.

Sinha's (1992) paper entitled 'Occupational Mobility in West Bengal with Special Reference to Moyra Caste' explains that in ancient period the profession of sweetmeat making was exclusively meant for the Moyra caste and they provided food to the orthodox Hindus. The Brahmins used to take water from them. When traditional occupations of the Moyras became unprofitable, as they were preparing the sweetmeat in the traditional way, they adopted different professions. Meanwhile, some members of other castes have adopted machines and modern technologies for the production of sweetmeat. The economic backwardness of the Moyras compelled them to work in such sweetmeat shops besides other vocations. At present, about 75 per cent of the other castes are engaged in this profession.

The paper on 'Occupational Mobility among the Harijans or Urban Bihar' by Sinha and Singh (1992) is based on the study of intergenerational occupational mobility among the five Scheduled Castes living in Patna town. The study has made occupational comparisons, between grandfathers and fathers, between fathers and respondents (the respondents belong to different age and income groups, but the majority of them, i.e., 63 per cent are below 40 years of age, and nearly 37 per cent of them are above 40 years), and between grandfathers and respondents. It is pointed out that mobility between grandfathers and fathers was not high, and in this category people were engaged in caste-occupations in greater number, whereas mobility between fathers and respondents was relatively more. The study concludes that, in Patna town, the traditional occupation of the castes has economic viability and gives good earning to those who cling to it. At the same time, it has been shown that the urban influence has enabled some persons to move from caste calling to non-caste calling.

The preceding review of literature has attempted to delineate only a few studies despite the fact that extensive studies on villages all over India have been conducted by a number of scholars. Srinivas (1942, '52, '55, '59, '62, '72, '76), Morris and Singh (1948), Dube (1955, '58), Majumdar (1958), Lewis (1958), Mayer (1960), Epstein (1962), Ghurye (1963), Ishwaran (1968), Madan (1968, '79), Sarkar (1971), Mann (1972), Rizvi (1974), Rao (1974), Misra (1974), Gupta (1975), Bose (1975), Cohn (1975), Singer (1975), Varma (1977), Hiramani (1977), Kundu

(1978), Gupta (1978), Ansari (1980), Subbiah (1981), Tsukasa & Tsuyoshi (1981), Nakamura (1982), Karashima (1983), Chakraborti (1983), Komoguchi (1984), Burman (1984), Gupta (1985), Morab (1985), Ekka (1985), Danda (1986), Datta (1987), Mukhopadhyay (1989), Mandal (1991), Sinha (1992), Sinha & Singh (1992), and others have conducted studies on various problems of Indian villages.

Kerala Villagae Studies

In Kerala there have been some studies on the village communities, Aiyappan (1965), Mammen (1975), Alexander (1975), Mathur (1977), Oommen (1979), Verghese (1986), Osella and Osella (2000) and others, which keep on the dynamic aspects of the village society. A number of studies on the heterogeneous population were carried out by a number of scholars (e.g. Fawcett (1901), Thurston (1909), L.K.A.K. Iyer (1909 & 1939), L.A.K. Iyer (1961), Schneider & Gough (1961), Fuller (1976), Jeffrey (1976), and others). Apart from this many works on the historical, political, socio-economic aspects, etc., have been done in Kerala.

An examination of the Census of India in 1961 resulted in the publication of a number 'Village Survey Monographs'. It was realised from the Census that, in a country, largely illiterate, where the statistical or numerical comprehension alone was felt insufficient, an understanding of the social structure was essential. This attempt was to put some "flesh-and-blood accounts of social structure and social change upon the dry bones of village statistics". In Kerala, thirty-five villages namely, Amaravila, Kadakkavoor, Kottukal, and Parassala in Thiruvananthapuram district; Edamon, Eravipuram, Thankasseri and Thazhava in Kollam district; Bharanikavu, Kadapra, Muttar and Prakkad in Alleppey district; Ankamali, Mulavucad, and Thekkumbhagam in

Ernakulam district; Kurichy in Kottayam district; Nemmara in Palakkaed district; Anthicad, Lokamaleswaram, Panancherry, and Thalikulam in Thrissur district; Cheruvannur, Muttil, and Naduvannur in Kozhikode; Edakkad and Thiruvangad in Kannur district had been surveyed in 1961. A few tribal villages such as Attapadi, Champakad, Chingeri, Kadukkamkunnam, Nilambur, Palode, Periyar, Thirunelly and Udumbannor had also been included in the survey.

Krishna Iyer (1961) made a monumental study entitled 'Kerala and Her People'. It explains the mode of living, occupation, taboos, marriage and rites of the autochthons of Kerala and their correlation to the most highly advanced groups. The study surveys the history and racial origins of the people of Kerala and explains briefly the social structure and economic life. The chapter on social structure deals with the origin of caste, caste in Kerala, and the future of caste. The author is of the opinion that, "the old economic life was based on the simple needs and habits of the people. The caste was the basis of economic structure. The wider dissemination of technical knowledge was responsible for changes in the hereditary nature of occupations. The application of science to industry is the pivot on which many changes revolve. The wide ramification and increasing specialisation in obtaining a living has brought to the fore certain stratification in society. The rise of business class with increasing opportunities for middlemen is a significant point in the changing economy of the State. The emergence of these classes modified the caste system and is a dominant strain in the changing pattern of the society, the occupational aspect of the caste system"(Iyer 1961: 163–64).

Aiyappan (1965), an eminent anthropologist of Kerala, made a study entitled 'Social Revolution in a Kerala Village'. Aiyappan (1905-1987) studied at the London

School of Economics under Professor B. Malinowski and Professor Raymond Firth. In 1982 he published another work entitled 'The Personality of Kerala', which traces the earliest roots of the culture of Kerala. The book deals with the archaeological and socio-cultural aspects, and a brief description of some castes and tribes of Kerala. It has mentioned the castes like Nambutiri Brahmins, Nayars, Temple servant castes, Izhavas [Ezhavas], Washerman, etc.

Mathur (1977) in his paper on 'Socio-economic changes among the Weaker Sections of the population of Kerala' explains the socio-economic changes among the Weaker Sections of Anjumoorthy, a multi-caste village in the Palakkad district. The Weaker Sections in Anjumoorthy belong to the Scheduled Castes and Backward Classes and constitute 75 per cent of the total population of the village. The study describes the economy of the Weaker Sections, and identifies them in terms of access to the control over the means of production, socio-political and religious institutions. Mathur also points out that though there has been a perceptible change in economic opportunities, some of the basic traditional structures still persist particularly among the Weaker Sections, Izhavas, Kammalas, Harijans and other serving castes. For instance, the washerman, barber and artisan castes even today discharge their traditional functions in the village. The paper has briefly explained the changes in the technology of cultivation, economic and organisational change, and political and ritual change.

Verghese (1986) has made a sociological study on the changing socio-economic and agrarian structure in Kuttanad, in Kerala. For Verghese, most of the changes have been brought about in the Post-Independence era through planned economic and social measures. The study was based on the data from eleven villages and fifty families from each village, and few castes and communities namely, Christians, Nayars, Ezhavas and Scheduled Castes. According to Verghese (ibid.: 89) social change has been slow in Kerala, especially in the Kuttanad region and this is partly due to the rigid caste system and partly due to the comparative imperviousness of this area to the Non-Hindu invaders. He says that, in all the eleven villages the upper-caste Hindus and a few Syrian Christians controlled the affairs of the villages. The study explains a number of aspects viz., education, transport and means of communication, population increase, labour problems, break up of the patron-client relationship, labour unions and the strength of Marxist and communist parties, problems of cultivation, etc. The study concludes that the social order of Kuttanad has undergone great changes. Untouchability is a thing of the past, but caste distinctions do exist. Inter-caste marriages are unpopular, but people are becoming more and more aware of tolerating other castes and creeds. Interdining is not uncommon and caste distinctions are replaced by class. In most matters, what is significant is money. Verghese also asserts that structural-functional analysis has been the theoretical basis of this study.

Alexander (1992), in his paper on 'Emergence of Agrarian Movements and Class Consciousness among South-Indian Peasantry', has examined the socio-historical process through which the agrarian movements have emerged in South Indian States, namely Kerala and Tamil Nadu, and the changes created by these movements in the consciousness of the peasantry. Alexander is of the view that the developmental process initiated by the Colonial Government and the Missionary activities created imbalance in the traditional equilibrium between the cultural pattern, wealth and power of different castes, provoking the lower sections to make their advancement. According to him, "Izhavas were one of the depressed castes who were mobilised to fight against social oppression and to achieve better status in the society. Izhavas were traditionally toddy tapers, and were treated as untouchables. They suffered many social inequalities. With the spread of education and change in the economic situation, they found their traditional condition unbearable. This led them to organise themselves under the banner of Sree Narayana Dharma Paripalana Yogam (SNDP), and to mobilise their members for the redressal of their inequalities. Similarly, Pulayas and other depressed castes also formed their caste organisations and mobilised their members"(ibid. 152).

The paper delineates the activities of the Malabar Tillers Association (1937), Travancore Agricultural Labourers Union (1939), Kerala Tillers Association (1956), Kerala State Agricultural Labourers Union (1969), Kerala State Agricultural Labourers Federation, National Agricultural Labourers Union, Kuttanad Agricultural Labourers Union, Farmers and Agricultural Labourers Association, etc. and these movements created a change in the traditional labourer-cultivator relations. The paper among other things describes the agricultural labourers unions of Tamil Nadu. It also discusses the changes in social relations, particularly the tenurial relations, and economic consequences. The study concludes that the mobilisation of the proletariat has brought together the poor, and led to the reorganisation of social relations, including property relations, heralding new egalitarian relations in the countryside.

E.M.S. Namboodiripad (1994) in his book 'The Communist Party in Kerala: Six Decades of Struggle in Kerala', gives a political account of how the party became the organiser of the workers and peasants and the pacesetter for the democratic movements. The book also deals with the political movements and efforts made in this direction from the time of formation of the first Kerala unit of the Communist Party of India in 1937 upto the

1990s. A short note on the change in agrarian relations has also been included in this book.

Osella and Osella (2000) in their book entitled 'Social Mobility in Kerala – Modernity and Identity in Conflict' describe the socio-economic change of the Izhavas [Ezhavas] of Kerala. It compares the social mobility of the Ezhavas with that of the Christian and Nayar communities. This study is essentially an ethnographic as well as analytic one and it gives a wide range of information including the present socio-political aspects of Kerala.

Bhanu and Mahendrakumar (2000) have made a village study, the Kottakkal village, in Malappuram District of Kerala. The study has identified the traditional and modern aspects of life and culture of the heterogeneous people comprising Hindu castes, the Christians and the Muslims. The study essentially points out some of the major socio-economic and cultural transformations that took place in the village during the 20th Century.

The preceding review of literature obviously points out that all villages and social structure of castes are changing. The change in the traditional caste based occupation is pervasive throughout the villages in India. Many castes have abandoned their traditional caste based occupations and adopted new ones. The occupational mobility within the caste and outside can be seen in this dynamic village life. In other words the occupational diversification sometimes provides occupational mobility within the caste or outside. In most of the cases, some socio-cultural and economic factors are involved, and this involvement often ranges from the silent obligatory relationship to the explicit conflicting community level of relationship. This tension and crises mostly open up new pattern of interrelationship in which people may or might have abandoned some traditional pattern of livelihood. Thus, new means of livelihood emerge and later they develop into occupational categories of people. This is the context of the present study of a Kerala village explained below.

Kerala Village

Major focus of the present publication is confined to a village and the occupational diversification, and socio-cultural change. This book provides the pattern of development of the village and the ideas about the positive trends of the development of the village. The book is hoped to be helpful for the planners, administrators and the development agencies. Further, it is expected that the study will also help initiate similar studies at a wider level. The area of study is the Vallachira village, in Thrissur taluk of Thrissur district, Kerala State, and 12 KMs south of the Thrissur town. The population of this village is heterogeneous, comprising different castes and communities.

Justification for the selection of the present village is that it provides both the critical changing aspects and the traditional aspects. The present delineation explores the process of occupational diversification and its impact and socio-cultural changes taking place in the village. Moreover, in spite of changes, some aspects like the traditional occupation are still persisting among some castes, and alongwith the occupational shift to non-caste occupations extensive shift of people to some caste occupations is also taking place.

Various anthropological methods like household survey, personal interview, participant observation as well as non-participant observation, case studies, and genealogical method have been used for the collection of data. The household survey was conducted for collecting information on village population, house types, family types, marital status and relationships, educational standards, caste, occupations, possessions, etc. By employing the genealogical method, the family types, inheritance pattern, and the demographic structures have been obtained. The non-participant observation, formal and informal personal interviews helped to gather adequate and in-depth information from the field. Informal interview and informal conversation have been held for specific purposes and focused on certain planned content areas. These methods were very helpful in understanding the nature of caste interactions, occupational problems, attitudes of the people appertaining to the present day change.

Originally, the first phase of the fieldwork of this study was conducted in 1994-1995 period. "Pilot studies are essential in order to foresee flaws and handicaps which might be encountered in the full-scale study" (Young 1966. 1992, rpt.: 25). In the first phase, the caste and community composition of the village was done. A qualitative appraisal was made, in the first phase, on the traditional and non-traditional occupations of the village people, which was helpful in understanding some features of the village as well as for undertaking the present study. The second phase of the fieldwork was conducted in 1998-99 period. The final phase of the fieldwork was done during 2000-2001 period. The data collected earlier were incorporated with the new data in order to make this study more comprehensive. Apart from this, I have been very careful to provide the facts and also to construe the findings correctly. Appropriate stress has been made in the analyses and presentation of the quantitative as well as qualitative data. Secondary data consisting of documentary sources supplementing and substantiating the field data were made use of from various official records, reports and documents. The Census, National Classification of Occupations (NCO), Gazetteer, Development Report of the Grama Panchayat, etc., were very valuable for the present study.

This book has six chapters. The first chapter, 'Introduction', consists of review of literature, which describes the nature and coverage of various village and caste studies conducted in India. The review obviously points out that the villages and castes are changing. The village life is dynamic; many castes have abandoned their traditional caste based occupations and adopted new occupations. In other words, the occupational diversification has resulted in occupational mobility within the caste.

The second chapter, 'Village Ethnography', gives a brief description of the village, the people, traditional occupations of different castes and communities. The present study is confined to a midland village called Vallachira village, which belongs to Thrissur taluk of Thrissur district in Kerala State. The population of this village is heterogeneous, comprising different caste and communities. The Nayars, Ezhavas, and Christians are the major castes and communities in terms of their numerical strength. In the village, there are thirty-five castes, subcastes and communities namely, the Nambutiri, Embrantiri (Cannada Brahmin), Pattar (Tamil Brahmin), Nambisan, Warriar, Marar, Nayar (Vellaima Sudran, Sudran, Pallichan, Vattekadan, Pillai, Menon, Kartha, Veluthedath Nayar, Velakkithala Nayar), Ezhuthachan, Ezhava, Ezhavathi, Nadar, Kalarikurup, Viswakarma ("Kallan" and "Tamil Thattan"), Marasari, Kallasari, Musari, Karuvan, Thattan, Pandaran, Kudumbi, Perumannan, Vettuvan, Pulaya, Paraya, Christians, and the Muslims. An attempt has been made in this chapter to identify the traditional occupations of all castes and communities inhabiting this village.

The third chapter deals with the Socio-Economic Structure of the village. The occupational diversification within caste and outside caste purview is also included in this chapter. Occupational shift is also analysed.

The fourth chapter delineates the 'Social and Cultural Interaction'. The differences occurred in the interaction pattern are also explained in the chapter. The structural functional theory of Radcliffe-Brown and the structural theory of Levi-Strauss are analysed and applied in this study. The failure of those theories to the new situation of society is an important finding.

The fifth chapter 'Pecuniarisation–A new theory of social change in India' provides the theorisation and analysis of social and cultural life. Contemporary social situation provides quite a different view and accordingly a new theory–Pecuniarisation–is framed. It also gives an overall picture of socio-cultural change evolved in the village due to occupational diversification and change. Impact of occupational diversification explains the after-effects of occupational diversification. The sixth chapter provides the conclusions and the summary of the findings.

2

VILLAGE ETHNOGRAPHY

The present study is conducted in Vallachira village belonging to Thrissur taluk, Thrissur district, in Kerala State. Thrissur district has an area of 3032 KM^2. According to Census 2001, the population of the Thrissur district is 2,975,440 and the total population of Kerala is 31,841,374 that comprises 15,468,614 males and 16,372,760 females. The altitude of the district is Sea level. Thrissur district is considered to be the "cultural capitol" of Kerala. Kerala Kalamandalam, a cultural centre as well as institute for teaching the renowned classical dance Kadhakali, the Kerala Sahitya Academy and Kerala Sangeetha Nadaka Academy are located in this district. The two longest rivers of the State, namely, Bharathapuzha and Periyar flow through the district on its northern and southern sides respectively. Gayathri is an important tributary of the Bharathapuzha. Heavy rainfall, warm humid atmosphere and almost uniform temperature throughout the year are the climatic features of the district. Guruvayoor township with the famous Sree Krishna temple, 29 KMs west of Thrissur, is one of the most frequented pilgrim centres of Kerala. The Thrissur Pooram festival is another attraction, which enjoys inter-national repute. Apart from this, the district is known for its gold jewellery business throughout Kerala and outside.

The district-wise strength of population has been furnished below. Actually, comparing the population with the area of districts in terms of the Census data may not be appropriate, since there exists difference in possession of area in each district. The geographical peculiarities and area of the districts are different; hence their carrying capacity will also be different. The Census 2001 also gives a general profile of sex ratio, growth of population and density of population of the 14 districts. Population-wise, Thrissur has third position in the State. Thiruvananthapuram district has the maximum population and Ernakulam comes next in density. Thrissur district is situated in the central part of Kerala. The villages show typical characteristics of Thrissur district, namely, the heterogeneous population, physiography, traditional economic structure, etc.

Table 1
District Wise Population Profile of Kerala

Sl. No.	*District*	*Area Km2*	*Population*	*Sex ratio 1991-2001*	*Growth rate*	*Density per Km2*
1.	Kasaragod	1992	1203342	1047	12.30	604
2.	Kannur	2966	2412365	1090	7.13	813
3.	Wayanad	2131	786627	1000	17.04	369
4.	Kozhikode	2344	2878498	1058	9.87	1228
5.	Malappuram	3550	3629640	1063	17.22	1022
6.	Palakkad	4480	2617072	1068	9.86	584
7.	Thrissur	3032	2975440	1092	8.70	981
8.	Ernakulam	2407	3098378	1017	9.09	1050
9.	ldukki	5019	1128605	999	6.96	252
10.	Kottayam	2203	1952901	1025	6.76	722
11.	Alappuzha	1414	2105349	1079	5.21	1496
12.	Pathanamthitta	2642	1231577	1094	3.72	574
13.	Kollam	2491	2584118	1070	7.33	1038
14.	Thiruvananthapuram	2192	3234707	1058	9.78	1476
	Total	38863	31838619	1058	9.42	819

Source: Census of India 2001- Kerala (Provisional).

According to the provisional list of Census 2001, the percentage of urban population is 25.97 and the remaining 74.03 per cent comprises rural population. The rural population factor is known as villagers. Therefore, the study of villages is an important area at present to understand the people of Kerala villages as well as the whole country. In Thrissur district, 72 per cent of the total population live in villages.

Table 2
KERALA: Rural-Urban Distribution of Population, 2001

	Male	*Female*	*Total*
Rural	11451282	12123167	23574449
Urban	4017332	4249593	8266925
Total	15468614	16372760	31841374

Source: Directorate of Census Operations, Kerala.

Table 3
THRISSUR: Rural-Urban Distribution of Population, 2001

	Male	*Female*	*Total*
Rural	1018315	1116484	2134799
Urban	403737	435696	839433
Total	1422052	1552180	2974232

Source: Directorate of Census Operations, Kerala.

The villages are classified on the basis of the strength of population. In some cases, one or more villages constitute a Grama Panchayat. The Vallachira village is a major part of Vallachira Grama Panchayat. The Vallachira Grama Panchayat comprises the Arattupuzha village and a small part of the Urakam village, apart from the Vallachira village. The Vallachira village has six *desam* or regions namely, Cherussery, Vallachira, Chathakudam, Perumpadappumcherry, Kadalassery and Urakam. The Arattupuzha village has three *desam* or regions, namely Arattupuzha, Pallissery, and Njeruvissery.

According to the Thrissur Supplement of the Kerala District Gazetteers (1981), the Vallachira village has an area of 14.88 KM^2. In the light of the Development Report of the Vallachira Grama Panchayat, the Vallachira village has an area of 631.4395 hectares. Vallachira is a multicaste village situated 12 KMs south of Thrissur town. It lies in between the Thrissur – Ernakulam National Highway 47 and Thrissur– Irinjalakuda State Highway.

Physical Features of the Village

Physiographically, the Vallachira village lies in the central midland region of the Thrissur district whereas the coastal villages of Thrissur district are comprised of lowland, the villages situated in the eastern part of the district are adjacent to the Western-ghat comprising highland. A hill, namely, *ilamkunnu*, having a height of 350 feet is situated on the southern part of this village. A big pond, the *Vallachira-chira*, is situated at the centre of the village. The major part of the north-west and eastern sides of the village are bordering paddy fields.

Climate

The village has a tropical humid climate, oppressively hot, and receives high seasonal rainfall. The hot season from March to May is followed by the south-west monsoon from June to September. October and November form the post monsoon or retreating monsoon, although the rain stops by the end of December, and the rest of the period is generally dry.

Rainfall

The south-west monsoon generally sets in during the last week of May. The annual rainfall is in between 3150 mm and 3180 mm.

Kerala State

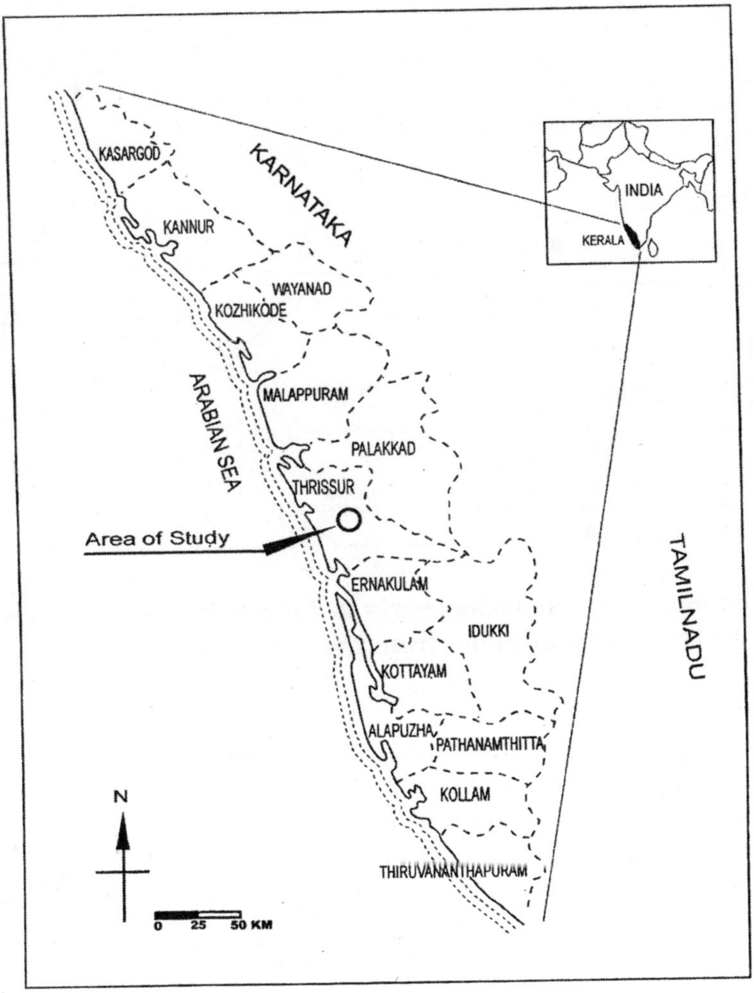

Temperature

By the end of September, after the end of monsoon, temperature, particularly in daytime, increases, and in the summer, it reaches upto 37° C. The weather is oppressive by hot in the summer. With the beginning of

Thrissur District and the Vallachira Village

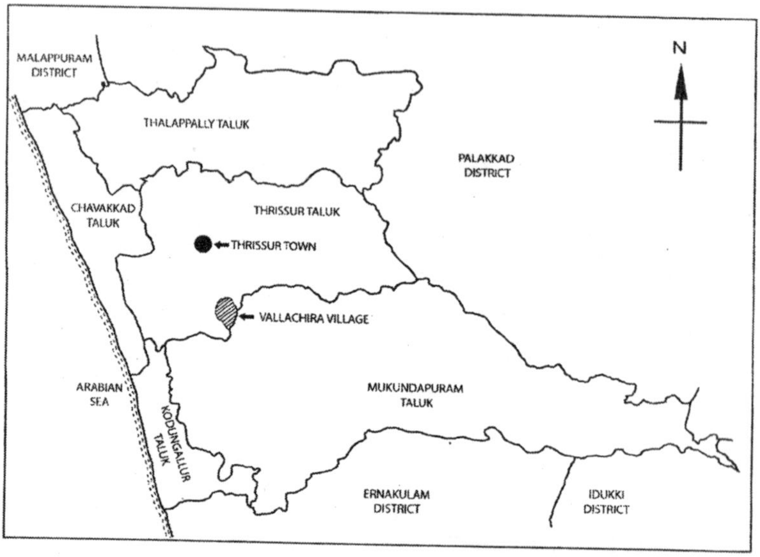

the south-west monsoon, early in June, temperature drops, and there is some relief from the oppressive heat.

Flora

The flora of the village comprises a number of trees and shrubs. Coconut trees, arecanut palms, mango trees, jackfruit trees, cashew nut trees, rubber, tamarind, banana, etc., are abundant in the village. Paddy, pepper, etc., are cultivated in this village. A number of trees belonging to wild varieties are also found. Besides, more than a hundred varieties of medicinal plants are also found in this village.

Fauna

Cow, buffalo, goats, dogs and cats are domestic animals reared by the people. Apart from this a number of birds, squirrels, rabbits, snakes, rats, frogs, fishes, etc., are found in the village.

Vallachira Village

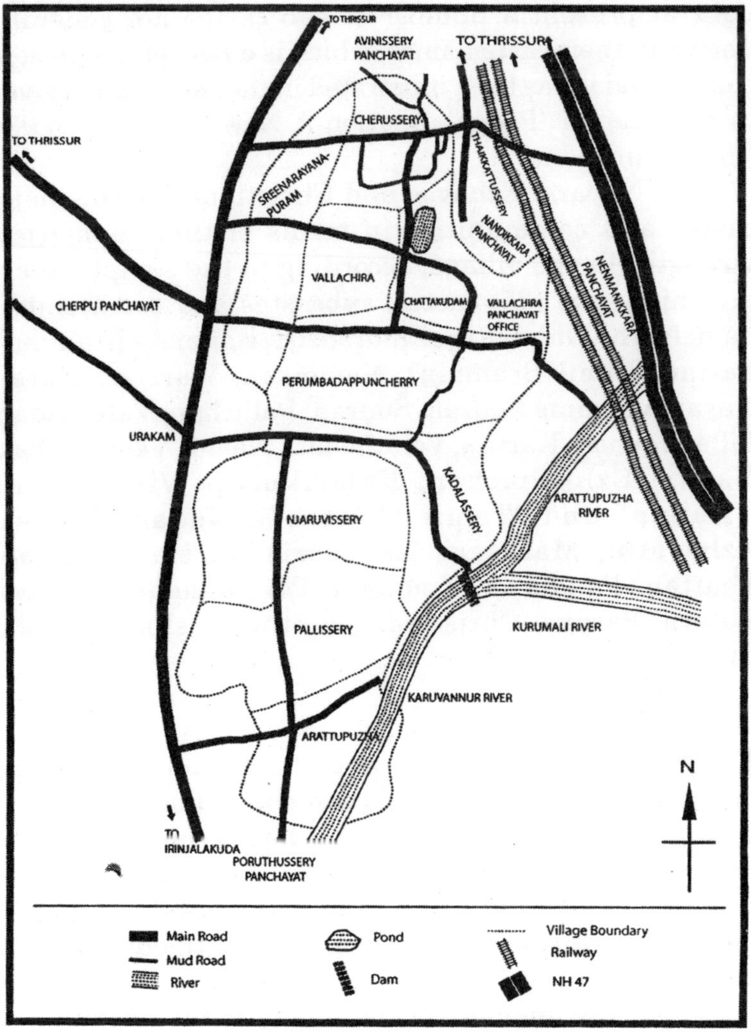

The People

The multicaste village provides a unique ethnic situation of Indian society and culture. The population comprises different castes and communities. Through the household survey conducted at the sub-caste level, it has come to light at present a number of sub castes are generally known in their caste names, which is a part of the present change and it has been illustrated in the caste fusion given in the chapter 'Pecuniarisation-A New Theory of Social Change in India.

The Nayars, Ezhavas and Christians are the major castes and communities in terms of their numerical strength. In the village, according to the sample, there are thirty-five (35) castes, subcastes and communities namely, the Nambutiri, Embrantiri (Kannada Brahmin), Pattar (Tamil Brahmin), Nambisan, Warriar, Marar, Nayar (Vellaima Sudran, Sudran, Pallichan, Vattekadan, Pillai, Menon, Kartha, Veluthedath Nayar, Velakkathala Nayar) Ezhuthachan, Kalarikurup, Viswakarma ("Kallan" and "Tamil Thattan"), Nadar, Ezhava, Ezhavathi, Marasari, Kallasari, Musari, Karuvan, Thattan, Pandaran, Kudumbi, Perumannan, Vettuva, Pulaya, Paraya, Christians, and the Muslim coinhabit there.

Nambutiris

The Nambutiris are a socio-culturally dominant and priestly class of people, who are characterised by their strong faith in God. They lead a highly spiritual life. A number of them are employed as temple priests traditionally. Earlier the Nambutiris were the *janmis* or landlords, who possessed a large part of the dry and wet land in the village.

The eldest member of the family is the *kaarnnavan* and he has absolute control over the property. Though earlier the younger members had no right over the property, at present all the members have equal right. Earlier, the eldest son alone was permitted to marry a Nambutiri girl whereas the younger brothers were permitted to have *sambandham* with Nayar women (Gough 1962). This situation has changed since and now all the members have the right to marry from the same caste.

The Nambutiris observed untouchability in the past but today particularly in this village, this has been reduced to a negligible extent. In many instances the Nambutiris show any nuances of untouchability and during religious and rituals they do not come in contact with people of other castes. The temple priests do not and should not touch people of other caste while engaged in the *pooja* or sanctification activities.

Embrantiris

The Embrantiris are the Kannada Brahmins, who have migrated from South Canara in Karnataka State and settled in Kerala. The Embrantiris are working as priests in temples traditionally.

At present, some of them are in business while the majority, particularly the older people are engaged in temples as *santhikkaaran* (priests). They also wear a sacred thread diagonally slung over their neck and shoulders. While performing *pooja*, they should keep a distance from people of other caste for maintaining purity. If a person of any other caste touches an Embrantiri, the latter must take bath, and only after that, he can continue the *pooja* or sanctification activities.

Pattar (Tamil Brahmin)

The *Pattanmar* (Pattars) are also known as Tamil Brahmins, who have migrated from Tamil Nadu and settled in various parts of Kerala. "Tamil Brahmins speak Tamil but they are not confined to TamilNadu. Having crossed the borders they are found in all the southern states" (Manickavasagam 1990:122). Though they know Malayalam very well, they also speak Tamil at home. They wear the sacred thread similar to that of the Nambutiris and Embrantiris. The women wear *chela*, which is a peculiarity of the Pattar women. Though the early generations of the Tamil Brahmins were proficient in the study of Sastras and Vedas, they have not been engaged in that tradition for a long time. At present, most of them are engaged in various services as officers and clerks in government and private sectors, bank employees, cooks, or working in the gulf countries, etc. Some of them have attained good education and in general, they have adopted all occupations, which provide them good income.

Nambisan

The Nambisan is a caste living adjacent to the Hindu temple in the village. They belong to the *Ambalavasi* group of castes. In general, the *Ambalavasis* have the privilege of doing service in temples. The family name of the Nambisan is known as *pushpothe*, and their traditional occupation is to collect *pushpam* (flowers), and making garlands for the temples. The Nambisan wears the sacred thread. In some other areas, they do not wear this thread. The Nambisan do not sweep the temples as they find it as a degenerate activity. The Nambisans bring flowers and garlands to the temples regularly according to the requirements. The service of making garlands is known as *maalakazhakam*.

In this area, there are only a few families of the Nambisans. The head of one of the families is still engaged in temple service. He has to provide flowers and garlands to the Shiva temple. In return, he receives a fixed remuneration from the temple.

Among the present parental generation, male members are known as Nambisans, whereas the female members are known as *Brahmaniamma*. These terms are added to their names as an honorific suffix, but among the present generation such terms are not suffixed.

Besides this the younger generations are not engaged in making garlands for the temples.

Warriar

The Warriar or Variyar belong to the *Ambalavasi* group of castes. They do not wear the sacred thread. They provide service to the village temples. The traditional vocation of the Warriars is cleaning the inner courtyard of the temples. In this village, the Warriars perform their traditional duty, whereas in other places they supply garlands too. The social status and hierarchical order of the Warriars are below the Nambisans. But in the neighbouring villages, there is no considerable difference. Earlier a Warriar could marry either a woman of the same caste or a Nayar woman. The Warriar–Nayar relation was known as *sambandham*. The male members of this caste are known as *Warriar*, and the female members are called *Warrasyar*.

The service in temples is referred to as *kazhakam,* and those who perform the service is known as *kazhakakkaar*. The cleaning service is known as *talikazhakam*. They have received good education today.

Marar

There are a few Marar households in the village. They are temple servants and drummers. Earlier, they relied solely on this occupation for their livelihood. They also play *panchavadya*. The word *pancha* means five and *vadya* means musical instruments. *Thimila, Suddha Maddalam, Ilathaalam, Kompu*, and *Idakkya* are the five musical instruments used for the *panchavadya* performance. In addition to the five musical instruments, a *sankh* (conch-shell) is also used for the *panchavadyam* performance. *panchavadya* commences with the blowing of *sankh* thrice.

In Cochin Census Report (1901), Mr. M.Sankaran Menon writes that the Marars are "sudras, and, properly speaking, they ought to be classed along with Nayars. Owing, however, to their close connection with services in temples, and the absence of free interdining or intermarriage with Nayars, they are classed along with Ambalavasis..." (Thurston 1909 (1975 rpt.): 7). The male members are known as Marar and the female members are known as *Aamma*.

Nayar

The Nayars are a numerically and socially dominant caste in this village. The caste name is also written as Nair. Most of the literature on Nayars (Fawcett 1901, Anantha Krishna Iyer 1912, Gough 1975, Fuller 1976, and Jeffrey 1976) provides the spelling as Nayars but in Kerala it is written as Nairs. In this book, I am following the transliteration of the pioneer scholars namely, Fawcett, Gough, Iyer, and others. The caste Nayar has a number of subcastes. But, at present, most of these subcastes are maintaining affinal and consanguineal relationship with each other. In the words of Krishna Iyer (1961: 46), "the Nayars were the first in the field of social reform. In 1901, there were 116 sub-divisions among them. In 1931, only two have been returned. It follows that the omission betakens change in social customs. The Nayars and the Izhavas or Ezhavas have removed all restrictions on intermarriage and interdining between subcastes, which they rigidly observed sometime ago". During the household survey of the present study, attempt has also been made to take the details of the number of subcastes in this area.

Vellaima Sudra Nayar

In the hierarchy of Hindu castes, the Nayars are positioned below the Ambalavasi group of castes and above the lower castes. The Nayars constitute a number of subcastes and the Vellaima Sudra is one among them. The subcaste

Vellaima Sudra is presently known simply as Nayars, and nobody is interested in knowing the subcaste among the Nayars with regard to the aspects of their socio-cultural living. Earlier the term 'Sudras' was used to refer to the Nayars, but it has ceased to exist today. The members of the subcaste Vellaima Sudra say that they are superior among the Nayars of this area. But it is also noted that the Kiriyathil Nayars, (the superior subcaste among the Nayars according to many scholars) do not inhabit this area. As such the Vellaima Sudras may be the superior one.

The Nayars, in general, followed *marumakkathayam* i.e., matrilineal law of succession. The eldest member of the family was the *kaarnnavan,* who was entitled to the full possession of their property. At present, both these systems do not prevail. The Nayars have now adopted patrilineal system. About their traditional occupation Anantha Krishna Iyer, (1912; 1981 rpt.: 97) has pointed out the following facts. According to him, "among the high caste Nayars, the recognition of caste by occupation is not possible. They were at one time a military caste, and as a relic of it, the small core of infantry maintained by the State is still known by the name of the ancient military caste of Kerala". During the feudal period, some among them relied upon land and at the same time a number of them were very poor. A few decades ago, a number of them were engaged in agriculture too. In the words of Anantha Krishna Iyer, (ibid.) the Nayars [of erstwhile Cochin State] numbered 1,11,837 at the last Census [1911], and of these, 28,786 are agriculturists". In addition, as per information gathered from the Nayars, they are agriculturists to a greater extent. During bygone days, this subcaste used to provide female servants to the houses of Nambutiris. Some families were engaged in agriculture alone. Presently they are known as Nayars or Nairs.

Sudra Nayars

At present, though the Sudra Nayars are known as Nayars or Nairs, the Vellaima Sudras of the village claim that the Sudra Nayars rank below the Vellaima Sudras. The difference is that the Vellaima Sudra Nayars were the Nayars working under "Vellanathu Mana", a Nambutiri family of early days. At present, they do not know anything about the origin and existence of that Nambutiri family.

Pallichan Nayars

The Pallichan is another subcaste of the Nayars, and are called Nayars. They are not known in the name of their subcaste. The old generation is aware of their traditional village life, very much unlike the present.

Traditionally, the Pallichan Nayars were the *pallakku* (palanquin) bearers of the Nambutiri Brahmins. A palanquin is a conveyance carried by men on their shoulders. When the palanquin became outdated, the Pallichan Nayars adopted other occupations.

Vattekadan Nayars

The Vattekadan Nayar is also a subcaste of the Nayars, and one family lives in this village. At present, they are known as Nayars, and the name of the subcaste is not used in the social context. The traditional occupation of the Vattekadan Nayars was pressing oil from *copra* (dried coconut) for temples and also for household needs. The elder members only remember their subcaste name. The young generation do not know anything about their traditional occupation.

Pillai

The word *Pillai* is the title of a group of families among the Nayars. They are engaged in modern economic pursuits in the changed socio-cultural situation. The Pillai is also known as a subcaste of the Nayars.

Menon

The Menon is a subcaste of the Nayars. *'Menon'* was a title given to many Nayar families and/or individuals by the then rulers of the erstwhile Cochin and Malabar States. The Menons were the accountants of the then revenue villages.

Kartha

The term *'Kartha'* is also a title given to some families and/or group of families among the Nayars. According to Anantha Krishna Iyer L.K. (1912 (1981 rpt.): 18), "the word [*Kartha*] means a 'doer', and appears to have been used as a title by some of the old Madura Kings. The rulers of Cochin are said to have conferred this title on some influential Nayar families, and made them petty chieftains subject to their paramountcy. All the Karthas belong to the *illam* division of the Nayar caste". In this area, there is only one family, which settled in the year 1983. At present, there are three members, viz., a widow, and her two daughters.

Veluthedath Nayar

The Veluthedath Nayars or Veluthedan is a subcaste of the Nayars and even now, they are known as the washermen and washerwomen of the Nayars, Warriars, and Nambutiris. The Veluthedath Nayars were matrilineal. The marriage ceremonies were not different from that of the upper caste Nayars. The Veluthedath Nayars did not wash the dress of the Ezhavas and other lower castes. Earlier, they were not allowed to use the ponds of upper castes. The upper caste Nayars did not marry women from a Veluthedath Nayar family. Today, marriages between the upper subcaste Nayar and the Veluthedan generally do not take place. The Veluthedans and the Velakkathalavans are classed under the group Sudras. Earlier, the touch of the Veluthedan was believed to pollute the upper subcaste Nayars. According to Anantha Krishna Iyer (1912; 1981 rpt.: 115), "though their touch pollutes the castes above them, the Nambutiris wear clothes washed by them without being in any way polluted, and the clothes washed by them are used even for dressing the idols in the temples".

Velakkathala Nayar

In the village, there are a few families of the Velakkathala Nayar. They are still maintaining their traditional occupation–hair cutting. Earlier, they provided their service to the upper castes only, but now-a-days they extend their service to all people irrespective of castes and communities. In general, the Velakkathala Nayars are also called as Nayars, but the upper caste Nayars do not have marital relationship with the Velakkathala Nayars. Like the Veluthedans, the Velakkathala Nayars also belong to the low caste Sudras. Earlier they used to visit the houses of the upper castes, one after another, for hair cutting. An old man, even today, visits the houses of all communities for providing his service.

Ezhuthachan

The Ezhuthachan is another caste group living in this village. Some call their men folk as *kadupattan* and the woman folk *pattathyar*. Anantha Krishna Iyer (1912; 1981 rpt: 104) is of the opinion that, the word 'Kadupattan' is another form of 'Kadur Bhattan' or Kadur Brahmans. They are said to have been banished from their country, the Chola Kingdom for favouring the introduction of Buddhism. They came to Kerala where they sought the protection of the Zamorin of Calicut, who allowed them to settle in his territory. "Ezhuthachan is a title originally given to the educated members of their caste by the senior lady of the Zamorin's family and other chieftains who subsequently authorised them to teach the low caste people. This points to their having been largely employed as village schoolmasters for a time" (ibid.). According to Thurston (1909; 1975 rpt: 209), Ezhuthachan means teacher or master of learning, and is the name for educated Kadupattans of Malabar employed as schoolmasters.

Krishnan Ezhuthachan, (1997) has pointed out, in his autobiography, that in order to abolish the caste name "Kadupattan" and to have them recognised as Ezhuthachan, the Ezhuthachan Maha Samajam, an association for the welfare of their own community was established in the first quarter of the 20th Century. The association has also attempted to remove a number of "irrational practices" prevalent among them. Earlier they were very poor, and many families have started agricultural activities for their livelihood.

Ezhava

The Ezhava is commonly known as "*chomaar*" in this village and neighbouring places. They are a numerically dominant caste group. The Ezhavas are placed below the Nayars and the Ezhuthachans. Earlier, the Ezhavas were respected by most of the lower castes. Some of the Ezhavas were agriculturists and some followed one of their traditional occupations such as toddy tapping. The Ezhavas were patrilineal and patrilocal. The caste organisation, S.N.D.P. (Sree Narayana Dharma Paripalana Yogam) has launched a number of activities for the welfare of the Ezhavas and it has virtually helped them to attain some development in their overall socio-cultural and economic spheres. There are sixty such households in this village, of which nine families are cultivating paddy for their own consumption, and the rest of them, irrespective of castes and communities, cultivate coconut trees. The traditional occupation of the Ezhavas was toddy tapping. In this village most of them have abandoned toddy tapping, and adopted various kinds of other occupations.

Ezhavathi

The Ezhavathi, known as Vathi or "barber", performed the religious rituals of the Ezhavas. They belong to the Other Backward Classes (O.B.C.) of Kerala. Some call them as "*Kuruppanmaar*". The traditional occupation of the Ezhavathi is generally known to be "hair cutting". Earlier they were not the "barbers" of the Ezhavas, but their priests. On the occasion of Ezhava marriages, the Ezhavathi priest had to provide garlands made of osimum leaves. It was given to the bride and bridegroom at the *pandal* where a *nilavilakku* (brass lamp) was lit and a measure of paddy kept near it in a bushel.

The Ezhavathi used to perform the *balikarmangal* (funeral rites) associated with the Ezhavas. When a man died, the Ezhavathi priest performed *pooja* (rituals) on the first day, and the Ezhavathi priest shaved off the beard of the eldest son and cut his "two hairs" on the sixteenth day. Later, they became the barbers of the Ezhavas. There was a period in which the Ezhavathi men and women used to visit the houses of the Ezhavas for cutting hair, and they received paddy or cash as their wages. The women cut the hair of women who were ill. Nevertheless, the women, mostly, were housewives. By the time the Ezhavas started discarding the priestly deeds of the Ezhavathi, some members opened barbershops for all castes and communities. Thus, at present, the Ezhavathi caste is popularly known as "barbers".

Hindu Nadar

The Nadars belong to the Other Backward Classes (O.B.C.) of Kerala. Their traditional occupation was toddy tapping from coconut trees. They were experts in preparing *tengin chakkara* (saccharine) from toddy. Lime is smeared inside the pot and kept for collecting toddy. Then toddy is boiled until it solidifies into saccharine. Though such saccharine is very sweet, one should not consume it alone, as it will cause minor inflammation in the mouth.

The Nadars of this village originally migrated from Trichy in Tamil Nadu and settled in Thalore, Konikkara and Eravakkadu (the neighbouring villages of the present area of study) in Thrissur district. About sixty years ago, one man started three toddy shops in the above villages, and for the purpose of tapping, he persuaded 60 families to settle in Kerala. The present families are the descendants of those families. Their position in the local caste hierarchy was below the Nayars and above the Ezhavas. It is better to mention that their social position is incomparable, since they were not the original inhabitants of Kerala. They claim that they performed the rituals similar to that of the Pattars and that is why some Nayars considered them as superior compared to the Ezhavas. The Nadars, however, did not marry from among the Ezhavas, though the traditional occupation (toddy tapping) was the same. According to them, whereas their relatives in Trichy practised uncle-niece marriage, the Nadar families of this village do not practice this.

Kalarikurup

In this village, the caste Kalarikurup is known as "*Panikkar*" or "*Panikkanmaar*", who are astrologers. They belong to the Other Backward Classes (O.B.C.). At present only a few of them practice astrology. Earlier, most of the elder members were experts in astrology, and some knew Sanskrit also. Some astrologers perform magic too along with astrology. They, however, lived in a miserable condition, and slog much for their livelihood. Therefore, they depend on diversified economic activities for their livelihood. At present, the trend has again changed. Astrology as a profession is prospering. Only the male members practice astrology. The male members are referred to as *Aasaan* and the female as *Panikkathiyar*.

Viswakarma

The Viswakarma is a caste, which came from Tamil Nadu and settled in various parts of Kerala. In this village, there are three households of the Viswakarma. According to Thurston (1909; 1975 rpt.: 412) "Viswakarma and Viswa Brahman are synonymous for Kammalans, the members of which class claim descent from the five faces of Viswakarma, the architect of the gods". Of these three Viswakarma families, one belongs to the subcaste "Kallan" and they are known as "Kallanmar". Their traditional occupation was making stone sculpture, stone lamps, grinding stones, etc. This family settled in the village about 50 years ago. Now they are not in their traditional occupation. The members of the other two families claim that they belong to the Tamil Viswakarma and their traditional occupation is goldwork. They claim that they are the Tamil Thattans but others call them as "Pandi Thattan". Both the "Tamil Thattan" and the "Kallar" speak Tamil in their houses. The youngsters, however, do not show any interest in their original mother tongue. Earlier they used to wear sacred thread but at present, they do not wear it regularly. However, they will have to use it for all rituals connected with marriages, death, etc. In the official records, both the subcastes are written as Viswakarma, and they are classified under the O.B.C. (Other Backward Classes).

Marasari

The Asari belong to the Kammalans, and the Kammalans are the group of artisans. They include the Marasari, Kallasari, Moosari, Thattan and Karuvan. In some places, it has been noted that the Chembootti and Kollan also belong to the Kammala group. In this village, I come across only the first five subcastes. The Asaris say that they originated from the Viswakarma.

The woodwork or carpentry is usually done by Marasaris. *Mara* means wood and *Marappani* is woodwork or carpentry, hence the name Marasari for carpenter. The role of the Marasari in the traditional set up is easily observable. The roofing of houses, furniture, and many other materials including the wooden plough are the products of the creative efforts of the Marasaris. Apart from this, in previous days the Asaris used to make large wooden granaries. In the words of Thurston (1909; 1975 rpt.), "the Asari ... is the Brahman of the Kammala castes. The Kammala castes generally pollute Nayars by approaching within twelve feet, and Brahman thirty six-feet, but an Asari with his measuring rod in his hand has the privilege of approaching very near, and even entering the houses of higher castes without polluting them. The exception may have arisen because of necessity". Only the male members do the carpentry, and the females remain as housewives.

Kallasari

The Kallasari is a caste traditionally engaged in masonry. They are different from the Marasari, since they are not engaged in woodwork. The Marasaris and the Kallasaris do not intermarry according to their tradition. Compared with the Marasaris, Kallasaris are a negligible few in this village. They are experts in making houses, compound walls, etc., with laterite slabs, bricks, and boulders. Only the male members are engaged in their traditional occupation. The female members are confined to the household activities. They follow patrilineal system from the earlier time itself.

Musari

There is a caste group called Musari who are the braziers. They make very attractive brass lamps, pots, vessels, etc. The production of these material objects requires the following steps. At first, moulds are prepared in clay, when it is dried, wax is coated inside the mould, and the melted brass is then poured into the moulds. Finally, the moulds are broken carefully, and the objects are finished or polished by using the traditional wheel mechanism.

The women also help in the preparation of bell metal objects. The women's role is to grind mud properly for shaping moulds, and rotating the wooden wheel while polishing. The men with various iron tools polish the objects kept on the wheel. The finished objects are sold to the villagers and to the shops in towns.

Thattan

The Thattan is quite familiar to all castes and communities. Their service is essential for all, since they are traditionally goldsmiths. The Thattans prepare gold ornaments not only for the people, but also for the village temples. They fabricate various kinds of ornaments using the minimum of mechanical devices. Earlier, from the design of the ornaments worn by a person, the identity of his caste was revealed. But, at present, there is no caste difference in the design of ornaments worn.

Although, they are working with gold, only a few families can earn money. Some families now make copper ornaments instead of gold ornaments. They sell these to those engaged in making rolled-gold ornaments. In this village, all the six families are engaged in their traditional occupation. Earlier, the Thattans were not engaged in any other occupations except jewellery making. In certain circumstances, women also help the men in making ornaments. They follow patrilineal system. At present, the Thattans experience tough competition in the field of jewellery making since many other castes and communities have adopted jewellery making as their major source of income.

Karuvan

The caste Karuvan is characterised by their proficiency in making iron-tools and implements. They are one of the Kammalans, and classified as Other Backward Classes (O.B.C.). The Karuvans are traditionally engaged in blacksmithy. They provide iron tools like sickle, knife, axes and implements for agricultural activities. They also undertake repairing of damaged bullock carts, though bullock carts are very rare today.

Usually the *ula* or smithy is adjacent to their houses and the Karuvan wife or children make the fire in the *Ula* while he himself manufactures or fabricates implements. All the agriculturists in the villages approach the Karuvan for various kinds of implements and their service is in great demand since they are the sole suppliers of such articles.

Pandaran

The Pandaran belongs to the Other Backward Classes (O.B.C.). Their traditional occupation is *papadam* (circular, curry wafers, fried for use) making. The fried *papadam* is an inevitable item for all the castes and communities. In bygone days, the Pandaran used to visit houses in the village for selling *papada.* Though these people are in the process of economic development, they still follow their traditional occupation, since *papadam* enjoys demand in the market. At present, people do not buy *papadam* directly from the Pandaran, because it is available in any grocery store. Besides, the Pandarans do not visit the houses of other castes for selling *papadam*.

Kudumbi

The Kudumbi is a bilingual community which speaks Malayalam and a dialect close to Marathi. They are categorised under the Other Eligible Community (O.E.C.). Thurston (1909; 1975 rpt.: 106) is of the opinion that, "the

Kudumis [Kudumbi] speak a corrupt form of the Konkani dialect of Marathi. They are the descendants of these Konkana Sudras, who emigrated from Goa on account of the persecutions of the Portuguese in the 16th century, and sought refuge along with their masters, the Konkana Brahmans, on the coast of Travancore and Cochin. Most of them set out as the domestic servants of the latter, but a few were independent traders and agriculturists". Even in the present day, the Kudumbi uses his traditional tongue at home. With the outsiders, they speak Malayalam fluently. The perpetuation of their language stems from the high group solidarity and cohesiveness among them. The female members use their traditional dress even today.

According to the members of the caste inhabiting the village, they had a traditional occupation namely, the preparation and sale of rice flakes. In Malayalam, it is known as *avil* (flattened rice). In former times they used to collect paddy from the villagers and after the preparation of flakes, they returned it to the donors who had given the paddy. Reciprocally, they received cash or paddy as wages. Earlier they had a particular kind of wooden mortar and pestle for flaking paddy, but now, some use modern motorised machine. A slow paced modernisation has taken place in their life.

Perumannan

The Perumannan is a Scheduled Caste called "Velan" and/ or "Mannan". The Velan and the Mannan are different subcastes, and in the past, there were no intermarriages between the Perumannan and the Velan or Mannan. The traditional occupations of the Perumannan are ayurvedic medical practice and washing clothes of the castes that are below the status of the Nayars but not below the Ezhavas. The men who practised ayurveda were known as *vaidyan*, and the women were known as *mannathi* i.e., washerwomen. The male members engaged in singing songs in the sacred groves for appeasing gods and goddesses as well as at the time of ancestor worship. Although the male members of the Mannans wash clothes, the Perumannan men did not wash clothes, as they are the *vaidyas* (doctors). Many of the *vaidyas* became experts in Sanskrit, since most of the books of ayurveda were in Sanskrit.

Mannathi-maattu was quite significant in the social structure of the bygone days. The acceptance of washed clothes by the higher castes, from the Perumannan woman, was known as *mannathi-maattu*. Even though the Veluthedath Nayars were the washermen and washerwomen of the higher castes, the Mannathi should provide *maattu* during delivery period, death, and other occasions where it had to overcome pollution. They should not give *maattu* to the lower castes below the rank of Ezhavas. In the course of the abandonment of the traditional occupation, the women left their traditional service of giving *mattu* for a long period. But they had held on to the occupation upto nearly two decades ago from now, whereas the men still follow their traditional ayurveda practice, which is based on the texts like Astangahrudaya, Sahasrayoga, Balachikilsa, etc.

Vettuvan

The Vettuvan is often mistaken as Pulayas, who were the agrestic serfs of Kerala. The Vettuvan belongs to the Scheduled Castes of Kerala. Some among the Vettuvans were agricultural labourer and some were the coconut pluckers. According to Thurston (1909; 1975 rpt.: 398) "they lead a hand-to-mouth existence on the wages which they obtain for hedging and fencing coconut plantations, plucking coconuts, tilling, and other allied work". The Vettuvans claim that they are superior to the Pulayas. Thurston (ibid.) has rightly pointed out that, "in point of caste restrictions they [Vettuvans] are certainly better circumstanced; and their daily contact with the higher classes in the ordinary concerns of the life affords them greater facilities for increased knowledge and civilisation than their brother citizen of the slave races enjoy".

In this village, the condition of the Vettuvans and the Pulayas is more or less same. Both of them are employed agricultural labour and fencing. A considerable number of them are coolies.

Pulaya

The Pulaya is a Scheduled Caste, and the name Pulaya might have been derived from *pulam,* which means agriculture field. The people who work in the field and live in or near by the fields were called Pulayas by the then dominant people. Most of the people belonging to the caste Pulaya are still continuing agricultural activities for their livelihood. Agricultural activities and their tradition are inseparable. Aiyappan (1992:38), is of the opinion that, "the slaves in Central Kerala are referred to as Cherumakkal, meaning minor or small subjects [people] among whom there are several castes such as Pulaya, Kanakka, Paraya, Vettuva". Earlier the Pulayas constituted the largest number of the predial servants and/or agrestic serfs. "The Sherramukkul [Cherumakkal] are attached to the glebe, but real property, in absolute market value not much above the cattle; united with them in estimation"(Ward and Conner, 1863; 1994 rpt.: 194).

Although they were kept away from the "mainstream" of the society, they had to perform their own role in the multicaste social conglomeration. They were traditionally engaged in agricultural activities and provided their services to the erstwhile land owning communities, mostly higher castes.

Paraya

The Paraya is also a Scheduled Caste inhabiting this village. Bhaskaranunni (1988: 259) is of the opinion that the caste name Paraya might have been derived from the word *para*, which means a musical drum. Customarily, they used to play a drum (*para*) in connection with marriage festivity as well as rituals connected with death of the Pulayas or related castes. Apart from this, the Parayas are known for their traditional service, weaving. Some of them are even now experts in making baskets, winnowing pan, mats, etc., using bamboo splits. In the past, they used to visit the houses of the upper castes with the bamboo products. According to Thurston (1909; 1975 rpt.: 77), "the Late Bishop Caldwell [Rev. Robert Caldwell 1814–1891] derives the name Paraiyan from the Tamil word *Parai*, a drum, as certain Paraiyas act as drummers at marriages, funerals, village announcements are proclaimed".

It has also been noted that some of their old members were experts in blackmagic. The present generation does not know anything about such practices. In the social hierarchy, they rank below the Pulayas. At present, they do not perform drumming either for their own marriages or for the marriages of the Pulayas. They follow patrilineal descent and patrilocal residence pattern. They have already discarded a number of age old cultural activities; nevertheless, a few in the neighbouring villages perform their traditional dance form, the *Parayankali* or *Darikanthullal*, during festivals.

Christian

The Christian community has become an integrated part of the village similar to many other villages in Kerala. The Christians in the village follow diversified economic activities. Although, there are many denominations among them, the Christians of this village come under the

Marpappa and are commonly referred to as Roman Catholics. They belong to the Syro Malabar Sabha, which is also known as Suriyani Sabha. The Catholic Sabha, originally, has two divisions namely the oriental and the occidental sabhas. The western division uses Latin whereas "the Romo-Syrians follow the doctrines and rites of the Roman Catholics, and they use a Syrian version of the Latin liturgy" (Thurston 1909; 1975 rpt.: 449).

Most of the Christians are traditionally engaged in agriculture, trade and conveyance. According to Anantha Krishna Iyer (1912; 1981 rpt.: 456), "the Syrian Christians are found in all grades of occupation; many of them are agriculturists, while others are engaged in trade."

Muslim

There are a few Muslim families in this village. It has been noted from some literatures that the Muslims are traders of all goods as well as labourers. However, some of them are agriculturists.

Population Structure

For a diachronic analysis, the customs and a brief history of castes, and the traditional occupations of all the castes, subcastes, and communities were identified. There are 35 castes, subcastes, and communities in this village. Some of the subcastes are not known by the name of their subcaste. For example, among the Nayars, there were some subcastes namely Vellaima Sudra, Sudra Nayar, Pallichan Nayar, and Vattekadan Nayars. However, today, these subcastes are not known by the name of their subcastes. They are simply known as Nayars. The other divisions such as the Velakkathala Nayars and Veluthedath Nayars are still known at the subcaste level itself. Besides this, the upper caste Nayars do not have marital relations with the inferior subcastes namely the Veluthedan and Velakkathala Nayar. At the same time, the Menon, Pillai, and Kartha are known by their respective titles. That is, in the case of some subcaste of Nayars, caste fusion has taken place, particularly in the upper subcaste level.

In some cases, even though the present caste name is one and the same, the traditional occupation and the traditional subcaste names are different. This can be found among the Viswakarma. Among them one group is known as "Tamil Thattan" and the other group as the Kallan. The Tamil Thattans are the goldsmiths, and the Kallans are the sculptors. Therefore, the present study attempted to explore the traditional occupations of the castes at the subcaste level. Table 4 shows the castes, subcastes and communities of the village.

Table 4
Households of Castes, Subcastes & Communities

Caste, Subcaste & Communities	*House holds*	*No.of Male*	*No.of Female*	*Total*
1. Nambutiri	6	14	10	24
2. Embranthiri	3	6	10	16
3. Pattar	7	17	11	28
4. Nambisan	2	4	3	7
5. Warriar	8	14	16	30
6. Marar	2	6	5	11
7. Nayar Vellaima Sudra Nayar	40	91	88	179
8. Sudra Nayar	9	27	23	50
9. Pallichan Nayar	16	28	34	62
10. Vattekadan Nayar	1	3	5	8
11. Pillai	1			
12. Menon	1	2	6	8
13. Kartha	1			
14. Veluthedath Nayar	12	38	38	76
15. Velakkathala Nayar	1	5	7	12
16. Ezhuthachan	18	47	39	86
17. Ezhava	60	144	156	300
18. Ezhavathi	1	3	1	4
19. Nadar (Hindu)	1	2	2	4
20. Kalarikurup	16	56	60	116
21. Viswakarma "Tamil Thattan"	2	12	13	25

Contd....

Caste, Subcaste & Communities	*House holds*	*No.of Male*	*No.of Female*	*Total*
22. "Kallan"	1			
23. Marasari (Carpenters)	19	62	69	131
24. Kallasari (Mason)	3	15	9	24
25. Musari (Braziers)	2	3	6	9
26. Thattan (Goldsmiths)	6	15	23	38
27. Karuvan (Blacksmiths)	3	8	6	14
28. Pandaran	2	5	8	13
29. Kudumbi	17	42	44	86
30. Perumannan	19	65	52	117
31. Vettuvan	5	8	9	17
32. Pulaya	21	64	50	114
33. Paraya	3	10	5	15
34. Christian	53	150	113	263
35. Muslim	1	2	3	5
Total Households	363	968	924	1892

In the foregoing pages an attempt has been made to draw an outline of the traditional occupations, services and duties of the castes, subcastes and communities of the village. A brief description of the typical features of each group has also been made. The enumeration of the total people gives the population structure of the village and the population details of each caste group and community.

The Table 5 shows the age and sex-wise distribution of the whole population. The total number of the people living in the village is 1892 consisting of 968 males and 924 females. The total number of the families is 363. The male outnumber the females. The maximum number of population comes under the age group 25–29 with 120 males and 112 females. The next population group, 202 members comprising 111 males and 91 females, belongs to the age group 20–24. However, as far as the females are concerned, the number of females just below the maximum number is similar in the age group 20–24 and 30–34, which consists of 91 females in each group. The age group 30–34 includes the third position in terms of females. The age group 10–14 includes 82 males and 83 females. The total number of the people in the age group 0–4 and 5–9 show that, the male-female ratio, probably, may exhibit the present situation of the total number of the people in the coming years also. Because, the age group 0–4 is comprised of 81 males and 61 females. Whereas, the age group 5–9 has 70 males and 61 females. That is, the number of males of the two age groups outnumbers the females of the same age group.

Table 5
Age and Sex-wise details of the People of the area

Age Group	*Male*	*Female*	*Total*
0 - 4	81	61	142
5 - 9	70	61	131
10 - 14	82	83	165
15 - 19	58	74	132
20 - 24	111	91	202
25 - 29	120	112	232
30 - 34	104	91	195
35 - 39	74	65	139
40 - 44	63	41	104
45 - 49	38	44	82
50 - 54	31	48	79
55 - 59	42	34	76
60 - 64	27	39	66
65 - 69	33	35	68
70 - 74	18	18	36
75 - 79	8	21	29
80 - +	8	6	14
Total	968	924	1892

The social conglomeration of the village provides the stratification of a variety of castes and communities. The numerically dominant communities have critical role in the decision making of the development and welfare of the village. The Ezhavas occupy the first position in terms of the numerical strength. The Nayars and the Christians have the second and third position according to the numerical strength.

3

SOCIO-ECONOMIC STRUCTURE

Even today, in India, the traditional occupational patterns of different populations are considerably based on caste system. Occupations possess the mode of economic activity of people and the studies of occupational structure portray the economic structure of villages. Earlier, the occupational structure was complex and rigid, and opportunities for occupational mobility or change did not exist as we experience at present. In the traditional set up, the members of each caste group had to perform specific functions, and that service and/or occupation was considered as the traditional occupation. "Generally a caste or a group of allied castes considered some of the callings as its hereditary occupation, to abandon which in pursuit of another, though it might be more lucrative, was thought not to be right" (Ghurye 1932; 1988 rpt.: 15). Madan (1979: 207) says "Nesfield regards occupation as the exclusive basis of caste distinction. Although this is not true in all cases as agriculture is followed by both higher and lower castes, there is some truth in his contention, for many of the castes followed a particular occupation and they were named after that occupation". Nevertheless, Mayer (1958; 1986 rpt.: 24) has rightly pointed out that it would be impossible to discuss any major aspect of the villager's life without mentioning his caste. The manner of the rites he performs, often his occupation, the kind of social and economic relations he has with his fellow-residents, all vary with caste membership.

The changes in the occupational patterns have been identified in the early decades of the 20th century itself. According to the Census Report (1931: 296), there was "a tendency of castes to abandon hereditary calling and take up others...and there was a similar tendency to give up caste calling for trade... A general examination of the castes tabulated by occupation enables the position to be roughly summarised as follows: In the majority of cases about half the males tabulated retain their traditional occupation and varying numbers upto, but rarely exceeding, a quarter, have other subsidiary occupations. About a quarter or less of the half that have abandoned their hereditary occupations as their principal means of subsistence retain them as subsidiary". Again, the same Census Report mentions that "in certain directions of course this tendency [i.e., the tendency of castes to abandon hereditary calling to take up others] has existed for long. Agriculture for instance is a respectable calling and it is one, which at any rate can be conveniently combined with many caste occupations. And the tendency to substitute agriculture for other pursuits must be of very long-standing and many castes whose names imply some other occupation are now turned agricultural. Possibly many have always been so, for the typical Indian village system, in which various occupational castes pursue their calling in a single village for the benefit of the whole village community, seems to be of comparatively late growth and is possibly the result of deliberate administrative arrangements".

The 'Occupational Information Unit' of the 'Directorate General of Employment and Training', 'Ministry of Labour, Employment and Rehabilitation', Government of India, have published the National Classification of Occupations (NCO) in 1958, and it has identified 2485 kinds of occupations consisting of non-traditional and traditional occupations all over India. The principle of "type of work performed" was adopted for the classification of occupations. The history of occupational classification dates back to 1946. That year the then Directorate published the 'Guide to Occupational Classification', and it was an industrially biased occupational classification, framed after the British pattern.

The Anthropological Survey of India conducted a study on the Indian population through the "People of India Project" which was started on 2nd October 1985 and according to it there are 4673 castes and communities in India. According to the Census, there are 427 Scheduled Tribal communities in India. India has the second largest concentrations of tribal population in the world. African continent is in the first position. The total scheduled tribe population in India is about 6.78 Crores which constitutes about 8.08 per cent of the total population of the country, excluding the population of the state Jammu and Kashmir where Census could not be operated for the disturbed situation. Apart from this, according to Census of India, there are six (6) major religions and 63 other religious persuasions in India. The six major religions and their percentages are as follows. The Hindus comprising of 82 per cent, the Muslim 12.2 per cent, the Christian 2.34 per cent, the Sikhs 1.94 per cent, Buddhist 0.76 per cent, and the Jains 0.40 per cent. But, the NCO could identify only 2485 kinds of occupations consisting of non-traditional and traditional occupations all over India. Due to extensive gaps in literature, it is a difficult task to correlate all the caste occupations of the people of India, at least for the present time, and it is also not the goal of this book.

The tendency for occupational change is essentially need-based and the occupational diversification may be due to several reasons such as to compensate for cyclical or seasonal fluctuations in demand and/or desire to maximise profits. In the words of Alexander (1992: 152), "the processes initiated by the colonial government, such as bureaucratic administration, rule of law, impersonal administration of justice, expansion of economy, improvement of technology, expansion of transportation and communication facilities, introduction of modern educational system, etc., sowed the seeds of change". After Independence, extensive plans and programmes administered by the Government of India brought about a series of changes in the Indian village communities. With the advent of industrialisation, the people could find new job opportunities in different areas other than their traditional caste bound occupations. This ultimately exposed the traditional vocational groups to new areas of life and culture.

Apart from this, since Independence, the Government of India realised the importance of rural development. Therefore, a number of development and welfare measures have been initiated in order to bring the rural masses into the mainstream of national development. The initiation of various welfare measures in the field of education, health, sanitation, family planning, housing and special welfare programmes for the Weaker Sections including women, Scheduled Castes, Scheduled Tribes and Backward Classes made it possible to improve the living standards of the rural masses including the poor. On the other hand, all these planned programmes were directly and indirectly diversifying the occupational scene. The diversification of occupations has strengthened the inter-caste, inter-village, village-town, and national and international relations. The communication skill of the people living in different socio-cultural levels also has improved. These changes are increasingly reflecting on the life-style of the people.

The caste bound traditional occupations reflect the social structure of Indian village. The pace of change of occupations or the means of livelihood is getting changed greatly in the villages. The present analysis is a diachronic one and it is limited to the time of Independence and upto the present day. Further, as far as the analysis of socio-cultural change is concerned, it is intended to trace the socio-cultural change in relation to the occupational diversification, and thus, the perspective of socio-cultural change is limited to the following areas such as the traditional occupations, services and duties of the castes, subcastes and communities of the village (area of study) in relation to the social and cultural characteristics of each group. The process of occupational diversification in terms of different castes and the factors contributed to the process of occupational diversification are analysed in this book. The structural and functional role of castes and communities in terms of their caste occupations, services and duties and the impact of occupational diversification on family, marriage, caste and community interaction, education, living standards, etc., are analysed.

The magnitude of socio-economic structure in relation to the occupational diversification of the village is quite important. The traditional occupation of the people of this village has been identified and dealt in detail in the previous chapter-village ethnography. The two aspects namely, 'occupation' and 'diversification' are the pivotal focus of the present chapter because occupations are economic activities and diversification provides new opportunities for economic activities. Originally, all occupations are certain economic activities, which are prescribed, developed, or adopted for livelihood. Occupation has great potential in life, because it is essentially an economic activity, without which survival becomes difficult. In the progressive stages of the eco-cultural adaptation, human activities have been changed extensively.

There are several meanings for the word 'occupation'. It means the state of being employed or occupied, the act of occupying, habitual employment, profession, craft, trade, etc. In the words of Rao (1994: 422) "the words work and occupation are often used interchangeably. In fact, occupation is essentially a kind of work. But, the word 'occupation' is used mostly to refer to the specialised and the established kind of work. It refers to some kind of work with which an individual becomes completely engaged. It denotes the habitual employment, profession, craft or trade of an individual. It takes up much of his time and attention. In modern connotations it means an instrument of livelihood. It is usually associated with one or the other kind of organisation, agriculture, industry, governmental organisation, etc. People pursue one occupation or other in order to eke out their livelihood. It has become an essential feature of the modern economic life".

The term 'diversify' means to make diverse or different, or to give variety to. *'Occupational diversification' can be defined as the development and/or proliferation and/or multiplication and/or diversification of occupations due to the introduction and/or adoption of new occupations into the existing occupations for novel social requirements.* Occupational diversification may emerge and/or is influenced by the reasons such as to compensate for cyclical or seasonal fluctuations in demand and supply and/or desire to maximise profits. In addition, occupations are modified according to human needs, when the existing social systems or network of social relations or social institutions fail to meet the existing requirements, or when new material wants are felt for a better living.

Occupation has also become determinant for the differentiation of separate human groups. The traditional occupations and services of the people of this village, like any other Indian village, are mostly caste-based. Therefore, the changes in the caste-based occupations are an important turning point in the social structure of the village life in India. The pattern of livelihood is essentially a major cultural determinant of the people, and it is guided by the occupations.

The traditional social structure of the villages in India is also based on the people and their institutions. The caste system was the determining factor of the occupations of people, and in every village, it is possible to observe the nuances of the traditional occupations, services, roles and duties of different caste groups. Ghurye (1986) is of the opinion that generally a caste group would have some hereditary callings for its traditional occupation and it was thought not to be right to abandon it. This view in turn shows the occupational rigidity of the traditional structure of multi-caste villages. According to Baden-Powell (1899; 1986. rpt.: 9–10), "every village [for him the term village includes both the cluster of houses and surrounding lands cultivated. Such a group has always a local name and known limits (ibid.)] is obliged to provide for itself the means of supplying the simple wants of life. The people could not go to a perhaps far distant town to buy shoes or find a carpenter; and hence they attract to themselves, and provide for, a little group (varying in different parts) of resident artificers and servants–a potter, a blacksmith, a cobbler, carpenter, washerman, sweeper, cattle-keeper, men to keep watch and ward, a barber to shave them… These servants live permanently in the village, and become hereditary…". In essence, in the villages, the extant of traditional caste based occupations was quite fervent, and almost all occupations, services and duties were explicitly appertained to some castes and communities.

Hiramani (1977: 10) is of the opinion that, "change in occupation or giving up of traditional occupation may mean change in the acceptable standard of living, change in values and ideology, or change in general circumstances in which livelihood is to be earned. Change in occupation while depending on these and similar factors itself gives an impetus to further changes in these factors. Thus, they are interlinked and interdependent. Need for a higher standard of living because of changes in outlook and values governing the style of life, new opportunities in occupations or component jobs in occupation resulting from the influx of technology and division of labour and opportunities in the acquisition of new sources of livelihood because of the changing socio-economic organisation in the village communities have been instrumental in introducing occupational change".

For the present study, the traditional occupations of the people are identified. The survey conducted reveals that only a few people are engaged in their traditional occupation. The extent of changes in their traditional occupations has also been analysed. At present, almost all castes and communities have adopted various new occupations instead of their traditional caste-based occupations. Nevertheless, some continue their traditional occupation. An attempt is made here to analyse the changes in the economic activities of the caste groups.

Among the Nambutiris, only a few members are engaged in their traditional occupation. Most of them are holding other jobs. They are working as clerks in Government departments and in the private sector. Some members are working in an ayurveda pharmacy, where drugs are prepared and bottled on a large scale. One boy is working as a mechanic in Mumbai, and another in a steel plant. An old man is engaged in agriculture and cattle rearing.

The Embrantiris are temple priests. They are working as *santhikkaran* (priest) in the village temple as well as temples in other villages. One of them is working in a hotel in addition to his traditional occupation. A family owns a hotel at Thrissur town and the members are also engaged in that business.

The Pattar is the Tamil Brahman and they are not in their traditional occupation. In the first decade of the 20th Century, it has been pointed out by Anantha Krishna Iyer (1912; 1989 rpt.: 338) that, "the priestly class of Brahmans and others proficient in the study of Sastras have, owing to the absence of sufficient encouragement, diminished in numbers, while others engage themselves in all occupations which afford decent income for their livelihood". The present survey reveals that they have adopted various kinds of economic activities for their livelihood. They are working in hotels, textile shops, bus services, gulf countries and in Government service, clerk in an ayurveda pharmacy, in catering service, in private companies, and in banks. At present, all the members have adopted various non-traditional occupations.

In the village, the Nambisan families are the people providing garlands to temples traditionally. Presently, only a few are engaged in their traditional occupation. The members are working as electrical wireman, and also working in an ayurveda pharmacy situated in the neighbouring village.

Traditional occupation of the Warriar caste is cleaning the inner courtyard of temples. At present, in the universe of study, nobody is engaged in their traditional occupation. However, two male members are engaged in temple service at the time of festivals. But in general, among the Warriar all members have taken up other occupations. They have good education, and many of them are employed in government and private sectors.

Traditional occupation of the Marar is drumming in temples especially during festivals. The families in the village are holding their traditional occupation. Some work as clerks in private companies, some are in gulf and others are employed in an ayurveda medical shop, etc., outside the village.

The Vellaima Sudra Nayars were servile to the Nambutiri families. Originally, the Vellaima Sudras associated with the works of the Vellayathu Mana, a family name of a group of Nambutiris, were referred to as Vellaima Sudras. As the social prestige is connected with the then masters of each caste, a group of families among the Sudras received a distinction as the "Vellaima Sudras" and they claimed that they were the superior group among the Sudras. Earlier some male members, referred to as *kaaryasthanmar,* used to supervise agriculture and other activities of the Nambutiri Brahmins customarily. The Vellaima Sudra women used to work as *pinaathi*, (maidservant) of the Nambutiri woman. The male members of the Vellaima Sudra Nayar were the seneschal or steward of the Nambutiri families. At present, nobody is engaged in this traditional activity. Nevertheless, an old man who worked as a clerk of an affluent *mana* (house of a Nambutiri) is alive.

At present, members of the Vellaima Sudra are engaged in highly diversified economic activities. They are engaged in various occupations such as agriculturist, oracle in temples, tea shop owner and employee, general merchant shop owner and employee, tile factory employees, drivers, goldworkers, *devaswam* (an official board of temples) employee, tailoring, plastic company employee, timber industry employee, electrical goods shop employee, carpentry, teachers, medical shop owner, ex-military, spinning mill and power loom employee, cooks for feasts, tyre re-treading industry employee, employees in ayurvedic medicine-preparing industry, ration shop partner, and coolie. Apart from these, some are clerks, stenographers and other employees at Chennai and Delhi. A few of them are working in various Government departments in Kerala.

The Sudra Nayars were also the steward of the Nambutiri Brahmins traditionally. In terms of the traditional occupation, there was no difference between the two subcastes. But the relative superiority of the Vellaima Sudras is due to their affiliation with the then affluent Nambutiri family. The Sudra Nayars are also, at present, not engaged in their traditional occupation. They have adopted diverse occupations, namely agriculture, cattle rearing, cook for feasts, coolie, tile factory, tailoring, ayurvedic medicine-preparing industry, welding workshop, business, goldwork and Government service.

According to literatures, the members of the Pallichan Nayar were the palanquin bearers. At present, the Pallichan Nayars do not follow their traditional occupation as it has disappeared with the kingdoms in Kerala. The present generation has embraced various jobs for their livelihood and they are as follows; agriculture, cattle rearing, hotel employee, ayurvedic medicine preparing industry employee, plastic company employee, coolie, goldwork, clerk in private sector, bank and other Government employment, teachers, tile factory employee, tea shop, welding workshop, sweeper in the village temple, and *combu* player (trumpeter).

Traditional occupation of the subcaste Vattekadan Nayar was pressing oil mainly for temples. There is only one family of the Vattekadan Nayar in this village. They are not engaged in their traditional occupation. The head of the family is a retired railway employee. Their eldest son is also working in the same department. The term "Pillai" is the title of a group of families among the Nayars. They are also engaged in diversified economic activities. The term "Menon" is a title given to some families of the Nayars who were the accountants of the revenue villages of the British India. Among the Menons, nobody is engaged in their traditional occupation. Kartha is one of the subcastes of the Nayars. "Kartha" is originally a title given to them. They are working as accountants in private business firm, etc.

The traditional occupation of the Veluthedath Nayars is washing the clothes of the upper castes. The men and women are known as washermen and washerwomen respectively. They do not wash the clothes of the castes below the rank of Nayars. Until a decade ago, they were engaged in their traditional occupation. At present, only a few families are engaged in their traditional occupation. Now, the very old people have given up their occupation on grounds of ill health. Today, only a few members are keeping their traditional occupation and the new generation has embraced diversified economic activities. Some are engaged in tailoring and of these one is in a gulf country and one is in Mumbai. Others are working in an ayurveda pharmacy, timber industry, tile factory, cycle repairing shop, coolie, auto driver through self employment scheme, goldwork, military service, and a few are in Government service. A few of them are working as mechanic in Mumbai, private business firms in the home town as well as in Delhi.

There is only one family of the Velakkathala Nayars. They are traditionally the barbers of the upper castes and they continue to follow their caste calling. At present a few members are barbers, and of these one has a barbershop in another village. Though they follow traditional occupation, one is a driver in the military service, and some women are engaged in tailoring.

Ezhuthachan, according to Anantha Krishna Iyer (1912), is a title given to the educated members of the caste group "Kadupattan", who were assigned the jobs of teaching the low caste people. But, the informants of this caste say that they were engaged in agriculture for their subsistence from time immemorial. In the village, nobody is engaged in the teaching profession despite having a few school and college teachers among them in the neighbouring villages. By practice, some of them were engaged in agriculture as labourers as well as agriculturists. Some were experts in ploughing the wetland with cattle and wooden plough. The present occupational status of the Ezhuthachan provides a number of occupations such as agriculturist, agricultural labourer, plough men, fertiliser depot employee, ration shop, tile factory employee, timber industry, mechanic in Mumbai, electrical wiremen, private company employee, co-operative society, postal department, news agency, medical shop, working in gulf countries, and also engaged in goldwork. As they were engaged in agriculture from time immemorial, the agricultural activities can also be considered as their traditional occupation. That is, the educated members work as teachers and others as agriculturists.

In olden days, the Ezhavathi were the priests of the Ezhavas and when they adopted hair cutting and shaving of the Ezhavas during the first quarter of the 20th century, it became the traditional occupation of the Ezhavathi caste. They also started new occupations other than their traditional occupation. In the sample, there was only one Ezhavathi family and the head of the family is practising traditional occupation, and he owns a barbershop in the village, but his son is in goldwork.

One of the traditional occupations of the Ezhava caste is toddy tapping. However, now most of them are engaged in diversified economic activities. Only one of the members continues their traditional occupation. Two persons are working in toddy shops and other members of the same families have taken up new occupations. In the sample, there are 60 households of the Ezhavas and of these 59 households have adopted diversified economic activities. Some are autorikshaw drivers, car and bus drivers, timber industry worker, carpentry, tile factory employee, tile factory partner, foot wear shop owner, goldworkers, loom worker, coolie, tailor, land broker, masonry, agriculturists, agricultural labourer, railway department employee, hotel employee and owner of hotel, rice mill labourer, electrical wireman and auto electrician, quarry business, Government employee, employees in private companies in the home town and in Calcutta, teacher of high schools, gulf, Kerala police and Tamil Nadu police, welding workshop owner and general merchant shop owners, employees in workshop in the home town and also at Coimbatore in Tamil Nadu.

The traditional occupation of the Hindu Nadar is toddy tapping. There is only one such family and the members are not in their traditional occupation. They have adopted other occupations. The head of the family is a hotel employee, and his wife is working in a timber industry.

Traditional occupation of the caste Kalarikurup is astrology. There are a number of households in this village. A few members are engaged in their traditional occupation. Now, most of the members have adopted other economic activities and working as agricultural labourers, timber industry labourers, carpentry, tile factory employees, house painters, loom workers, industrial estate employees, goldworkers, plastic company workers, general merchant shop owners, printing press owners, owner cum worker of PVC bend manufacturing unit, painters/artists, dance teacher, auto drivers, and private company employees in Delhi and Mumbai.

Among the Viswakarma, there are two subcastes namely "Kallan" and the "Tamil Thattan". Both these caste groups are presently known as Viswakarma. The traditional occupation of the Kallan is making sculpture by stone, whereas, the traditional occupation of the "Tamil Thattan" is making gold ornaments. The "Tamil Thattan" continues their traditional occupation, since it has great demand. The "Kallan" do not follow their traditional occupation. At present, all the three households are engaged in goldwork. Most of them are engaged in goldwork, but a few are working in timber industries as labourers, coolie, and some are working in gulf countries.

The traditional occupation of the Marasari is carpentry, and a number of them are engaged in their traditional occupation. Only one family has given up carpentry. There is one person who undertakes both carpentry and masonry. There are 35 members in 17 households engaged in carpentry. Nevertheless, a few of them are in diverse occupations. Three women are working as agricultural labourers, and in the off-season they undertake other works in the village. Some are brush company workers and some are coolies. Some work as clerks in private company at Thrissur, Palakkad, and also at Bangalore. Some have adopted goldwork and women doing tailoring. A few of them are working as carpenters in gulf countries.

The Kallasari is traditionally engaged in masonry. At present, they are engaged in masonry, tile factory jobs, goldwork, and a few of them are employed in gulf countries. The Musaris are the traditional brazier. Now, an old man is only practising their traditional occupation, the bell metal work or making brass vessels, etc. His son and the head of the other household have entered into goldwork.

The Thattans are traditional goldsmiths, and most of them are engaged in their traditional occupation. In the village, all of them perpetuate goldsmithy. Apart from this, some of them are working in the gulf countries. A few women work as tailors.

The caste Karuvan is the traditional blacksmiths of the village. Some of them have adopted new occupations, and are working as agricultural labourer, coolie, tailor, workshop worker, gulf employment, and goldwork.

Traditionally, the members of the caste Pandaran are the *pappadam* makers. We know almost all people in Kerala relish *pappadam* along with their meals and feasts. *pappadam* is a preparation with black gram flour and the thin circular shaped *pappadam* is fried in coconut oil and consumed along with meals. All the members used to make *pappadam* till recently. At present, a few of them have adopted non-traditional occupation for their livelihood, and therefore, nobody calls them by the name *Pappada Pandaran*. The village has now a few *pappad* makers, but some are goldworkers, printing press owner cum printer, timber industry employee, and carpentry.

The Kudumbis were traditionally engaged in making and selling rice flakes. Some also worked as agricultural labourers for their livelihood. In the sample, nobody is now engaged in making rice flake. However, some of their relatives living in the adjacent places are engaged in their traditional occupation despite having adopted modern machinery for the production of rice flakes. The present occupations of the Kudumbi are as follows. Agricultural labourers and coolie, tile factory employee, lorry driver, tea shop, quarry worker, coconut plucking, general merchant shop, and goldwork.

Among the Perumannan, which is a Scheduled Caste, the men and women had separate traditional occupations. The men were traditional mediciners (ayurvedic) and most of them had the knowledge of Sanskrit. Some male members have adopted magico-religious practices along with ayurveda treatment. A few male members were also engaged in *Thottampaattu*, a ritualistic event where songs are sung. The traditional occupation of the Perumannan women was washing soiled clothes of the Ezhavas and the Christians. The women had some rights in the households of the upper castes particularly at the time of pollution and they must give washed cloths (*mattu*) in order to remove pollution. The women of the village abandoned their traditional occupation decades ago. However, the men continued their traditional occupation as it has some demand. At present, only a man discharges his service as traditional *Vaidyan* (mediciner). Two others, in the line of the traditional occupation, are attached to the ayurvedic treatment, but not through the traditional line but in the modern line. Employment in the private sector in the home town and also at Delhi, mechanic at Delhi, Government employees, school teachers, ex-military, bank employee, engineer, doctor, tailors, and goldworkers.

The Vettuvan were agrestic serfs, traditionally engaged in coconut plucking, fencing, paddy cultivation, coolie, etc. Even today, most of them are engaged in their traditional occupation. A few of them have adopted new occupations. Among the Vettuvans, men and women were engaged in their traditional occupation, but obviously women do not climb trees to pluck coconuts. The non-traditional occupations of the members of this caste are namely, housemaids, timber industry labourer, watch repairing, and goldwork.

The Pulayas are the erstwhile agrestic serfs of Kerala. From the time immemorial, they were attached to *pulam*, meaning agricultural field. Pulaya meaning the people engaged in agricultural activities. Even at the time of Independence, the Pulayas were mostly engaged in the agricultural activities of the village. Despite many developmental activities designed to ameliorate their living, a majority of them are halfway down the development. The number of people engaged in their traditional occupation is more than that of those who had adopted non-traditional occupations. Some of them are coolie in timber industry, employees in paper cone industry, bamboo fencing, tile factory employee, carpentry, wood cutter in an ayurveda pharmacy, Government employment, boiler operator in the industrial estate, tailoring, goldwork, general merchant shop owner, and private company employee at Bangalore.

The Paraya caste members were traditionally engaged in weaving bamboo products. They used to visit the houses of agriculturists for supplying basketry items, namely, winnowing pan, baskets, bamboo mats, and a number of other such products. There are only three families of the Parayas, and nobody is engaged in their traditional occupation. The present generation is not interested in their traditional occupation, as it does not provide substantial income for their livelihood. The present generation has entered into various other occupations viz., agricultural labourer, timber industry labourer, coolie, auto driver, and also in Government employment. At present, the diversified economic opportunities provide them a number of jobs, however majority of them are working in the agricultural sector.

The Christian community follow diversified economic pursuits. Among the Christians, there are many denominations. The Christians of this village come under the Marpappa and are commonly referred to as Roman Catholics. Most of the Christians traditionally were engaged in agriculture, trade and conveyance. The concept of traditional occupation, virtually, is not applicable to the Christians and the Muslims. The people of the community have adopted various occupations, since there was no restriction for change of occupations as prevailed in the caste system. The present occupations of the Christians are namely, agriculturist, agriculture labourer, coolie, tea shop, cattle rearing, housemaid, baking, and general merchant shop. A few of them are timber industry labourers, tile factory employee, lathe workshop owner, automobile workshop owner, automobile shop employee, garment shop owner, jewellery shop owner, gold covering industry owner, goldworkers, ration shop, plastic company worker, paper cone industry labourer, tailoring, carpentry, house painters, private company employee in Mumbai, gulf, bank employee, teachers, ex-service men, vegetable vendor in the Thrissur market, and drivers.

In the village, there are a few Muslim families follow diversified economic activities. The Muslims are traders of all goods as well as labourers traditionally. Some are agriculturists. But, the concept of traditional occupation cannot be applied to the Muslims. Now they have entered into various economic activities.

It is understood that some castes have completely detached from their traditional calling, whereas in some other cases new occupations and their traditional calling go side by side. All the caste groups have adopted diversified occupations, and there is not even a single caste group, which completely depends on their traditional occupation. The total number of the traditional and non-traditional occupations of the castes and communities provides very significant picture.

The data show remarkable variation as far as the traditional occupations and non-traditional occupations of the people of the village are concerned. There are 92 households of different castes and communities engaged in their traditional occupation. Of the 363 households, 271 households have absolutely abandoned their traditional occupations. The total number of people as per their occupational status is 792; i.e., 792 members are engaged in various jobs including traditional and non-traditional occupations. Of these, only 151 members are engaged in traditional occupations or their own caste/community occupations and the remaining 641 members are engaged in non-traditional occupation.

It is important that the traditional occupation of a caste is the traditional occupation of that specified caste; meaning that the traditional occupation of a caste is not the traditional occupation of another caste. For example, carpentry is the traditional occupation of the Asari, who are the carpenters traditionally. Again, the Thattan are the traditional goldsmiths, and goldsmithy is their traditional occupation. Carpentry and goldsmithy are traditional occupations but carpentry is not the traditional occupation of the Thattan, and goldsmithy is not the traditional occupation of the Asari, despite the fact that both these occupations are traditional occupations of the people of this village. The traditional occupation is the caste occupation of the respective castes and communities. But, the non-traditional occupation includes the traditional as well as non-traditional occupation, that is, the number of non-traditional occupation includes the occupational shift towards new/modern occupations as well as towards the traditional occupations of the other castes, etc. Thus, we get a clear picture of the number of members following their own caste occupations. The number of households of each caste and community and the number of households continuing their traditional occupations are also important. The occupational shift of households from the traditional caste based occupations to other occupations is also analysed.

At present, almost all castes have adopted new or caste-free occupations, whereas members of some castes have adopted the traditional caste occupations of other castes. In the context of urbanisation and modernisation, the former pattern of adoption of occupation is common throughout India. But, the latter case is very particular as some caste groups have adopted the traditional occupation of other castes and this is an instance of occupational mobility within caste occupations.

The modernising process and improvement of the already existing traditional occupation are also a common phenomenon. For example, in the former days the goldsmiths used simple technology for the production of ornaments, but at present they use advanced mechanical devices for the production.

In compliance with the household survey, temple priests, garland makers, sweepers in temples, drummers, accountants and managers of Nambutiris, dobby, barber, teachers of lower caste people, toddy tappers, astrologers, goldsmiths, sculptors and grinding stone makers, carpenters, masons, braziers, blacksmiths, pappadam makers, rice flake makers, ayurveda practitioners, agricultural and horticultural labourers, weavers of basketry items, and those engaged in trade and conveyance were the major traditional occupations prevailed in the village for a long period. That is, in the traditional set up, there were 22 categories of occupations only, that were absolutely attached to 29 castes and communities in the village.

Originally, there are 22 traditional occupations, but some other activities like that of agriculturists, agricultural labourers, cattle rearing, *combu* player (trumpeter), cook for feasts, *Devaswam* employee, orator of the village temple, *para* procession, ploughmen, and toddy shop employee are listed under traditional categories of occupations. Further, although the trade and conveyance were the traditional activities of the Christian community, they were engaged in un-specific activities for their livelihood. At present, the following categories of traditional occupations and non-traditional occupations have been continued or adopted by the people of this village.

In the light of the survey, the number of members engaged in the traditional category of occupation is 372, whereas the number of members engaged in their own respective caste occupation is 151. That is, 221 members belonging to various castes and communities have adopted the traditional occupations of other castes. This number gives the dimension of the occupational shift within the castes and communities.

Occupational Diversification within Caste Occupations: A Case Study

Occupational diversification taken place within the purview of caste is a significant aspect as it can be considered as an index to the change of caste restrictions and ideology. Some examples for occupational diversification within the caste occupations are as follows. The caste Vettuvan did coconut plucking traditionally apart from the agricultural and horticultural activities, but at present some members of the Kudumbi are also engaged in plucking coconut. Some members among the Pattar and Nayar are engaged as cooks for feasts, and it is not identified as a traditional occupation, even though there were/are some families who follow(ed) cooking for feasts as their major activity for livelihood. Making copper ornaments was not common and it was not popular among the Thattan, but recently a family is also engaged in the making of copper ornaments for the gold covering industry, and this category of occupation is also classed among the traditional category of occupations.

There is a Nayar family which has the right of the service of an orator in the Bhagavathi temple of the village and this activity also cannot be identified as a traditional occupation, though this right has been transferred from father to son of a particular Nayar family. Besides this, some members of the Nayar caste participate in the *para* procession of the temple during the festival season, and this occupation also cannot be identified as the traditional occupation of the Nayars. Some members of the higher castes like Nayars have received jobs in the Devaswam, a body for the administration of the temples.

Among the Ezhuthachan, the educated members were the teachers who used to teach the lower castes, and some members were engaged as agriculturists, but in recent times some members are ploughmen, though this occupation cannot be explained as the traditional occupation of the Ezhuthachan. Among the Ezhava, some members are working in toddy shops and this was also not the typical traditional occupation of the Ezhavas though they are the traditional toddy tappers.

Although the traditional occupations comprise 22 major categories, some slight variations have occurred during the last few decades. In certain cases it could be referred to as occupational diversification but in some other cases of the traditional occupations it has not been identified as an independent traditional occupation. For example, cattle rearing has neither been identified as a separate occupation nor it a traditional occupation of a caste group in this village. In most of the affluent houses there will be one or two cows, and some sell the milk whereas some consume it.

In the case of agricultural labourers, the Pulaya and Vettuvan were engaged in this category of occupation for a long time in this village. But, during the last three-four decades, some members of the castes like Ezhava, Kudumbi, Christians, etc., also have started to work as agricultural labourers. Thus there are agricultural labourers, agricultural labourers cum coolie, agriculturists, and agriculturists-cum-agricultural labourers. This sector has been diversified considerably.

Agriculture and agricultural activities are the significant occupational sector as well as the means of livelihood of the villagers, as some paddy fields are situated in this village and its surroundings. In the light of the survey conducted, there are 12 caste groups and a community engaged in the agricultural sector as agriculturists, agricultural labourers, agriculturists-cum-agricultural labourers, and agricultural labourers-cum-coolie. They are namely, Nambutiris, Vellaima Sudra Nayar, Sudra Nayar, Pallichan Nayar, Ezhuthachan, Ezhava, Kalarikurup, Karuvan, Kudumbi, Vettuvan, Pulaya, Paraya, and Christian. Apart from this, some castes are also cultivating paddy and horticultural crops but they cannot be considered as persons engaged in agricultural activities even if the family members help at the time of cultivation. That can be referred to only as secondary occupations, and most of them have their own other (primary) occupations. In this village, the castes Pattar, Warriar, and Perumannan have cultivable land and they rely on the labour of the traditional agricultural and horticultural labourers whereby this category can be placed under the caption of cultivating group; however, cultivation is only their secondary occupation.

In essence, as far as the agricultural land and agricultural activities are concerned, some families of castes such as Nambutiri, Sudra Nayar and the Pallichan Nayar have agricultural land and they continue as agriculturists. Some families of the Ezhava, Ezhuthachan and the Christian community have agricultural land and they continue as agriculturists and agricultural labourers.

Some families of the Vellaima Sudra Nayar and Kudumbi have agricultural land and they live as agriculturists, agricultural labourers and coolie; whereas some families of the Pattar, Warriar, and Perumannan own agricultural land but no family members are engaged primarily in the agricultural practice. They rely completely on the traditional agricultural labourers for their cultivation.

In this village, there are 10 castes and a community having agricultural field and they cultivate paddy. The traditional agricultural labourers are working for the landowners and the caste Pulaya and Vettuvan are the traditional agricultural labourers and coolies in the village. The landless agricultural labourers belonging to the village, they are namely, the Kalarikurup, Karuvan and the Paraya caste inhabits the village. Originally, these three caste groups had their own traditional occupations, namely astrology, blacksmithy, and basketry respectively. It is obvious that only the affluent families of some castes possess agricultural land. In most of the cases, some of the family members are also found engaged in agricultural labour along with the hired labourers, mostly traditional labourers. But, the landless non-traditional agricultural labour can be considered as the occupational shift of the non-traditional labourers to the area of work of the traditional labourers. Further, if we take the number of agricultural labourers, the castes and communities like the Kalarikurup, Karuvan, Paraya, Kudumbi, Vellaima Sudra Nayar, Ezhuthachan, and Christian are engaged as agricultural labourers. Thus, six castes and a community have adopted the traditional occupation of the traditional agricultural labourers.

As far as the occupational shift is concerned, it has taken place in seven caste occupations namely goldsmithy, coolie, carpentry, masonry, agricultural labourer, cleaning the village temple, and *combu* (musical pipe) trumpeter. Earlier, it was a shameful activity to accept the traditional occupation of the other castes, but the present survey shows that a considerable number of the people are ready to accept any occupation, which provides stable employment and monetary benefit. Here, in this village, 19 caste groups have entered into the traditional occupation, goldwork, of the caste Thattan. The castes and communities engaged in goldwork are namely, Vellaima Sudra Nayar, Sudra Nayar, Pallichan Nayar, Veluthedath Nayar, Ezhuthachan, Ezhava, Ezhavathi, Kalarikurup, Viswakarma (Kallan), Marasari, Kallasari, Musari, Karuvan, Pandaran, Kudumbi, Perumannan, Vettuvan, Pulaya, and the Christian.

There are eight castes, sub-castes, and communities, which have adopted coolie as their main livelihood. They are namely, Vellaima Sudra Nayar, Sudra Nayar, Pallichan Nayar, Veluthedath Nayar, Ezhava, Viswakarma (Kallan), Marasari, and the Paraya. Apart from this, a number of castes and communities have adopted agricultural labour. The Vellaima Sudra Nayar, Ezhuthachan, Kalarikurup, Karuvan, Kudumbi, Paraya, and the Christians also adopted agricultural labour as their occupations.

The observation shows that the occupational shift has taken place within the caste occupations. The goldwork is the traditional occupation of the Thattan and 145 members belonging to 18 castes, sub-castes and a community have adopted this occupation as a primary occupation for their livelihood.

The coolie is virtually attached to the Vettuvan and the Pulayas, but 19 members belonging to eight castes, sub-castes, and communities have become coolies. The Pulayas and the Vettuvan are the traditional agricultural and horticultural labourers, but there are 25 members belonging to seven castes, sub-castes and communities who have become agricultural labourers.

The vocation carpentry is the exclusive service of the caste Marasari, but 10 members belonging to five castes and a community have entered into this occupation. According to the caste system, the Warriars are supposed to clean the inner courtyard of the temples, but a member of the sub-caste Pallichan Nayar, presently known as Nayar, has entered into this service. In essence, 200 members of 19 castes, sub-castes and a community have adopted the traditional occupations of 5 castes. This number reveals the stature and significance of occupational shift, which is taking place in a multi-caste-bound village. Although a number of castes and communities have adopted the traditional occupations of other castes, yet some castes have not entered into the traditional occupations of other castes. The Nambutiri, Embrantiri, Pattar, Nambisan, Warriar, Marar, Nayar (Vattekadan), Pillai, Menon, Kartha, Velakkathala Nayar, Nadar (Hindu), Viswakarma ("Tamil Thattan"), Thattan, and the Muslims did not adopt the economic activities of any other castes. In general most of the higher castes adopt the occupations of other castes.

It has already been pointed out that goldwork is the traditional occupation of the Thattan, but 145 members belonging to 18 other castes, sub-castes and a community who have adopted this occupation as a primary occupation for their livelihood. At present, 51 goldwork units are extant in the village and this "household-industry" has virtually developed into an occupational sector similar to industries that provide non-caste occupations. At present, goldwork has become a kind of household industry devoid of the status of a caste occupation. It is also peculiar that of the six families, only one of the traditional goldsmiths is having a multi-member goldworking unit. The development of this industry took place in 1980s. During the last two and a half decades, 64 members from various castes have entered into this job. Besides this, 140 workers from neighbouring villages are also working in these goldworking units, and they vary from single member unit to 15-member units.

There are 420 members of 35 castes, subcastes and communities who have embraced modern or caste free occupations. This figure shows the pattern of occupational shift from caste to non-caste occupations as well as occupational diversification within and outside the villages.

Occupational Shift Outside the Caste Occupations

The occupational shift outside the caste occupations that is from caste occupations to non-caste occupations is a general phenomenon, which is taking place extensively throughout India after Independence. The present survey also reveals the occupational shift towards non-caste occupations in the village. There are 31 categories of traditional occupations in the village and 372 persons are engaged in them; whereas 420 persons have received non-traditional or modern occupations. Non-traditional categories of occupations are of 98 kinds, and a number of occupations are available outside the village and even outside the State.

Development of Non-caste Occupations within the Village: A Case Study

The development of non-caste occupational ventures within the village can be attributed to the result of occupational diversification, which is nothing but the process of the occupational diversification itself. The development of non-caste occupations in the village has virtually taken place with the advent of small scale and cottage industries in the village as well as in the neighbouring villages. The advent of some Timber industries and Tile factories positioned in the pivot of the ventures provided non-caste as well as non-traditional occupations within the village, and the picture is similar in the neighbouring villages too up to some extent.

There are 48 shops, industries, and business establishments in the village alone, which provide non-caste occupations. In the decades before and after Independence, there were only two general merchant shops. In 1966, a ration shop were added. In the decade 1970 to 1979, there came up 8 more establishments. During 1980 to 1989, nine other establishments came up. It was in the year 1990 to 1999, that the maximum number of industries and establishments came up. Even in the year 2000, two ventures were started in the village, and this shows the increase in industrialisation and opportunity for occupational diversification. Altogether, there are 22 kinds of establishments started in the village since

Independence. It must be pointed out that people within and outside the villages started these establishments.

In the early phase of the development of non-caste occupations within the village, agriculture attained a very significant position in the village. Many people including the agricultural landowners, the traditional labourers and landless non-traditional agricultural labourers, etc., were attracted by and subscribed to the agricultural activities. The agricultural sector alone provided opportunity for the villagers to move from their traditional occupation to other sectors. In spite of the fact that there existed the traditional agriculturists and traditional agricultural labourers, most of the villagers were adapting themselves to the requirements of the agricultural sector. During those days the agricultural activities were quite traditional and the technology employed was rudimentary. They used cattle and wooden-plough, etc., for tilling the wetland, and sowing the seeds, harvesting, etc., were completely relied on human labour. But, after 1950s, they started a rice mill, which functioned by oil engine instead of electricity. Till that time the people used to husk of paddy with the use of wooden mortar and pestle. That is, the first mechanisation in the agricultural sector took place in the case of rice, the staple food of the villagers.

Along with the fulfilment of food requirements, shelter became a significant necessity for the people. Therefore, tile manufacturing also started in the village. This picture is more or less similar in the neighbouring villages, namely, Cherpu, Ollur, Nenmanikkara, Urakam, etc. Earlier, all the stages in the production of clay-tile were based on human labour alone, but by 1960s some tile factories introduced improved methods of production by means of mechanisation. At present, there are 12 tile factories having large-scale production and 25 small-scale decoration-tile manufacturing units established in the village. 630 labourers comprising 250 males and 380 females are engaged in this sector according to the Vallachira Panchayat Development Report (1996).

The advent of timber industries in the village by 1970s opened another avenue of employment and helped the people to have wood cut according to their requirements for constructing houses. The mini-industrial estate, which was established in this village in 1976 under the Industrial Department, also provided various opportunities for the villagers.

The process of occupational diversification is a significant aspect as it has the potential to alter the economic fabric of the village gradually or abruptly. Therefore, the present analysis of the process of occupational diversification will be helpful for understanding all the developmental activities of the village

In essence, there are two major areas for the process of occupational diversification, namely, (1) The occupational shift within the caste occupations, and (2) The development of non-caste occupations within the village. The occupational shift within the caste occupations has some limitations as the caste occupations are related to the cultural levels and status in the social conglomeration.

In the early decades, despite the society having been active in the struggle for abandoning some "irrational practices", which were considered to be against a secular State, the magnitude of occupational shift within the caste occupations was very limited. In the early decades, particularly after Independence, the people's aspiration was to have more caste-free occupations. Apart from this, people realised that they needed more facilities for their basic needs such as food, cloth and shelter. It was the industries, which provided more non-caste occupations for the villagers than the government sector. The businessmen within and outside the village started the non-caste occupational ventures. All these are the determining factors of socio-economic change of the village, and the same pattern is available in many villages in Kerala.

4

SOCIAL AND CULTURAL INTERACTION

This chapter analyses the structural and functional role of castes and communities in terms of their caste occupations, services and duties. It also explores the caste and community interaction, and the differences that have occurred in the interaction pattern. The use of the phrase 'structural and functional role' needs a precise explanation, as the terms 'structure' and 'function' have ample theoretical connections, and the use of which was popular in the recent past. As the present study is a diachronic one, some of the analyses stretch to the early concepts like 'function', and 'structure'.

The present day interaction pattern of the villagers is quite different from the earlier pattern. The functions and roles of castes and communities of the village have also transformed critically. Although this is a phase of radical changes in the village life, almost all people are identified through their caste and community levels in many circumstances, particularly in the village life. For example, if an outsider enquires about a person of the village, it is very common that the villager would ask the outsider which is his caste? or whether he belongs to this or that caste. The role of different castes and communities determines their position in the caste hierarchy and social sphere. Sometimes it becomes manifest whereas on some other occasions it is latent within the society. The social manifestations of the cultures of the people are based on the structure of the society. In the empirical level, the traditional caste occupations, services, and duties provided special sanctions and prohibitions. The role of each caste group is based on the hierarchical order and the positions of each caste. "The components or units of social structure are *persons*, and a person is a human being considered not as an organism but as occupying position in a social structure" (Radcliffe-Brown 1976: 10-11). "The social relationships…are determined by the social process, and any relationship is one in which the conduct of persons in their interactions with each other is controlled by norms, rules or patterns…The established norms of conduct of a particular form of social life it is usual to refer to as *institutions*. An institution is an established norm of conduct recognised as such by a distinguishable social group…The institutions refer to a distinguishable type or class of social relationships and interactions" (ibid).

In the words of Radcliffe-Brown (ibid.11-12), Social structure is an arrangement of persons through the institutionally controlled or defined relationships… Process is dependent on structure and continuity of structure is dependent on process…function is used to refer to the relations of process and structure. Keesing (1981) has provided an interpretation for the term 'interaction'; it is the "social behavior in which two or more individuals communicate and respond to one another's behavior." According to Radcliffe-Brown (1976:178-179), the concept of function applied to human societies is based on an analogy between social life and organic life. The life of an organism is conceived as the *functioning* of its structure. It is through and by the continuity of the functioning that the continuity of the structure is preserved.

Bohannan and Glazer (1973) defined function as the social function of a socially standardised mode of activity, or mode of thought, as its relation to the social structure to existence and continuity of which it makes some contribution. For Radcliffe-Brown (1976), the concept of function involves the notion of a structure consisting of a set of relations amongst unit entities and the continuity of the structure being maintained by a life process made up of the activities of the constituent units. "Function is the contribution an element makes to the whole social system. The difference between Radcliffe-Brown and Malinowski is...that Malinowski started with the individual. Individual needs were incidental to Radcliffe-Brown, who regarded the system of human interactions rather than human beings as being central in a functionalist approach to society "(Bohannan & Glazer 1973: 296). According to Turner (1979: 132) functionalism should not be viewed as a theoretical explanation. Rather, it will be more useful to the social sciences as a heuristic device and methodological tool that can assist theorists using less problematic theory building strategies. The three fundamental and connected concepts namely, 'process', 'structure' and 'function' were proposed by Radcliffe-Brown for explaining his structural-functional theory.

The term "structure" refers to a kind of organized arrangement of parts. In the social structure these parts are individual persons who participate in social life, occupying statuses in the social network. The social network is made up of social relationships between individuals of a society, who are controlled by norms or patterns (Bohannan & Glazer 1973: 296).

In every society, there are social relationships and each individual is socially controlled by certain institutions and associations. These act in a coordinated manner. There are different role groups in the society and each group has its own responsibilities and function to perform. The most important bases of social organisation are sex, age, kinship, social status, political power, occupation, religion and magic, totemism and voluntary associations. The family is the unit of social organisation in the villages. Most of the needs of males and females are fulfilled in the family. These families may be of different types such as nuclear family, joint family, etc. But, as the families of the village are based on different castes and community, a mere elucidation of family would not show the total picture. It is necessary to know the structural basis of the village. It has rightly been pointed out by Srinivas (1962: 44); according to him, "the structural basis of Hindu society is caste, and it is not possible to understand Sanskritization without reference to the structural framework in which it occurs." But it has to be pointed out that the process of Sanskritization has also resulted in the change of inter-caste and inter-community relations.

The service relations provide the interaction pattern. The change in service relations can be analysed by the identification of change in interaction pattern. One sector of the society receives services whereas the other sector renders services. The service relations of the people is more significant because the whole socio-cultural as well as economic status and characteristic of the village is based on the service relations, occupations, and duties of castes and communities.

Ainapur (1986: 67) has mentioned a remarkable aspect in his study by pointing out "if a high caste member has to perform certain duties in respect to a low caste family, he seems to be favouring them by his act. When a low caste member renders any service to a high caste family, he performs a duty. Such is the understanding between the persons actually involved in such relationships." This is a matter of construal, and it is essentially emic in nature. The disparities in service relations and the rules of social proximal distances were more fervent in the bygone days, and it has considerably declined at present. There are many reasons for the change. The change of the interaction pattern is abundant with the profiles of the downturn of the traditional socio-cultural elements of the village life. Inter-caste and inter-community relations or interaction have quite a lot of dimensions.

The social structure of the village is based on the inhabitants of the villages. As far as the present study is concerned, dynamic continuity of the structure is a formidable aspect for data and analyses. However, the significant turning point of the transitions is analysed. The fundamental nature and the pattern of social interaction in the village have utmost importance today.

Interaction: Traditional versus Modern

Though there are a number of castes, sub castes and communities, the Twice-born castes, the Ambalavasis, the Nayars, the Ezhavas, and the castes belonging to the lower hierarchical level, such as the *Kammalar* are the major groups of people in the village. The numerically dominant people may not be the ritually dominant caste groups. The Nayars are the numerically dominant caste group. The Ezhava occupy the second position in terms of their numerical strength. The third position is for the Christian community. The artisan castes, i.e. the *Kammalar* occupy the fourth position. In terms of numerical strength, the Brahmins and the Ambalavasis occupy the fifth and sixth position respectively. But, the Brahmins are the ritually dominant caste group and the Ambalavasis come below the Brahmins.

According to Srinivas (1966:10) "for a caste to be dominant, it should own a sizable amount of the arable land locally available, have strength of members and occupy a high place in the local hierarchy. When a caste has all the attributes of dominance, it may be said to enjoy decisive dominance. Occasionally there may be more than one dominant caste in a village and over a period of time one dominant caste may give way to another. This...has been an important aspect of rural social change in the twentieth century". Srinivas (ibid.) further says, "New factors affecting dominance have emerged in the last eighty years or so. Western education, jobs in the administration and urban sources of income are all significant in contributing to the prestige and power of particular caste groups in the village". However, Hasnain (1991: 227) argues that "due to immense expansion in transport and communication village level dominance is no longer enough to make a caste dominant caste". These are the different views of the dominant caste. And the conceptual framework of dominant caste itself shows a dynamic view, and it shows dissimilar changes. As far as a cultural milieu is concerned, the numerical strength of a population would reflect in the overall socio-economic status of that particular milieu. Therefore, a difference and peculiarity in emphasis and style in the interaction pattern also could be observed.

Nevertheless, the interaction pattern of the castes and communities is not completely based on the numerical strength; on many occasions, it is because of the particular traditional occupation or service of a caste. For instance, the Nambutiri Brahmin enjoys a higher position within the society mainly due to priesthood and the temples. The Nayars and the Ezhavas are the numerically dominant castes but they do not enjoy a position like a Nambutiri. But, in the present context, the traditional services and occupation and their change have exerted critical transformation in the interaction pattern.

Twice-Born Castes

In the traditional set up, people of the higher caste did not interact with the lower caste people as they did within their caste. Untouchability was also observed even in the first quarter of the 20th Century. But, when untouchability was abolished, the patterns of interaction changed considerably. At present, untouchability has completely disappeared from the social scene; however, it is preserved in some of the ritual matters pertaining to temples. Even today, the Nambutiri Brahmin should not touch the people belonging to other caste or community on or before the sanctification rites related to temples. If a Nambutiri priest (*Poojari*) touches a man belonging to another caste, the priest has to take bath to continue the *pooja* (sanctification rites) in a temple. The twice-born castes, in general, observed pollution strictly. The interaction of the Nambutiris is confined to the people belonging to the higher castes.

The Nambutiri, the Tamil Brahmins and the Kannada Brahmins are the twice-born castes in the village, and they are in the apex of the caste hierarchy. Today, the social interaction has improved greatly, and there is no explicit intolerance between the castes and communities. Modern education also paved the way for socialisation. The transport and conveyance system have also helped to reduce the social distance between castes and communities.

Ambalavasis

The Ambalavasis are also known as *Antharalar*. They are the service castes of temples. The castes Nambisan and Warriar are the Ambalavasis of the village. In the surveyed sample, the Warriar have completely abandoned their traditional occupation; however, both these castes continue their traditional calling and the service relations. Interaction of the Ambalavasis with the other caste people was very limited in the traditional structure but as they entered into many other occupations, they interacted with almost all castes and communities according to their modern occupations.

Nayars

The role of Nayar was one of coordinators of many activities between higher castes and lower castes. Nevertheless, some sects of the Nayars had to confine to a limited area of life and culture within the local caste hierarchy, which was purely based on the traditional occupation and/or services of the subcastes among the Nayars.

The subcastes, namely, the Pallichan, the Vattekadan, the Veluthedan, and the Velakkathala Nayar were purely service castes. The Subcastes Pallichan and Vattekadan do not exist today after the caste fusion has taken place among the Nayars as a part of social reforms, which attained momentum in the early half of the 20th century. The Veluthedath Nayar, that is the Washerman, still provides their service to the upper castes within and outside the village. The Velakkathala Nayar, the Barber, provides their service in the traditional pattern and started saloons within and outside the village.

Parallel Occupations

Parallel occupations were quite common during the last few years. There were two different Washerman castes namely the Veluthedath Nayar and the Perumannan. The Veluthedath Nayar should wash the clothes of the higher castes and should not wash those of the lower castes, whereas the Perumannan normally washes the cloths of the castes that positioned in the middle of the caste hierarchy. They should not wash the clothes of the lower castes. They should not wash the clothes of the Asari, Karuvan, Thattan, Pulaya, Paraya, and Vettuvan. They used to wash the clothes of the Ezhavas, Ezhuthachan and the Christians, generally. Nevertheless, earlier, they had to provide clean clothes known as *maattu* even to the Nambutiris for purifying pollutions connected with death, birth, menstruation, etc. Normally, the Veluthedath Nayar washed the clothes of the Nambutiris, and the Ambalavasis.

Hair cutting is another parallel occupation. The Velakkathala Nayar and the Ezhavathi do hair cutting. Earlier, the barbers belonging to the former caste provided their service to the higher castes only, and the latter provided their service to the lower castes. At present, both these caste groups not only provide their service to almost all castes and communities, but also continue their service as it has ample demand.

Ezhava

In this village, the Ezhava occupy the second position in terms of their numerical strength. Most of them were agriculturists and a few are attached to their traditional toddy tapping. They interact with the higher castes as well as lower castes in connection with the agriculture practice. They have some opportunities for interacting with the Nambutiris occasionally. At present, since they have entered into the diversified occupations they interact with every caste and community.

Kammalar Caste Group

The term *Kammalar* is used to refer to denote a group of castes, namely, Marasari, Kallasari, Musari, Karuvan, Thattan, etc. The services of the *Kammalar* are an inevitable one to anyone irrespective of caste and community. In the traditional set up they had an extreme importance because there were no other people to provide the kind of services they were providing.

Carpentry was an exclusive service of the traditional carpenters, the Marasari or "Asari". It requires good practical skill to make various wooden items. Their service varies from the supply of wooden spoon to various other wooden materials for the construction of all types of houses for the villagers. They make furniture such as table, chair, cot, stool, bench, cupboard, shelf, etc. Apart from this, their service is inevitable for the construction of houses, because woodwork is a major part of the traditional as well as modern types of houses. In the traditional types of houses, the roofing is usually done with wooden rafters and clay tiles. The architectural beauty and the strength of the wooden structures are based upon the materials used as well as the accuracy of construction and assembling. The houses, temples, etc., were constructed by the traditional carpenters. Earlier there was no mechanisation in the manufacture of wooden items but now they have started using electric cutter, router, drill, planer, etc. Today, some other castes also have adopted the traditional occupation of the carpenters because carpentry is in great demand. Though the carpenters are experts in the field of woodwork, the timber business is in the hands of the businessmen belonging to the other communities.

Now, though there are other caste people providing carpentry and masonry work, in the traditional set up the services of the Marasari, the carpenter, and the Kallasari were inevitable to construct houses. "Sub-castes within many of the occupational castes bear names derived from the special branches of the occupations" (Ghurye 1988:37). For instance, the Kallasari is the mason. In Malayalam, the word '*kal*' means laterite and the Kallasari are the traditional experts in the construction of houses using laterite; similarly, the word '*mara*' means wood and Marasari is the name of the caste group who work on wood.

The service of the Musari for providing brass lamps, vessels, pots and other items was very important in the traditional set up. But, at present, the use of brass pots and vessels has declined with the advent of steel, aluminium, and plastic pots and vessels. Besides this, people have started buying necessary items from shops instead of approaching the Musari of the village. This "consumer culture" has conquered the life and culture of the villagers.

The Karuvan, who are the traditional blacksmiths, provide a number of iron tools and implements to the villagers. The implements like *katthi* (knife), *vettukatthi* (cutter), *kaikkottu* (spade), *pikkas* (pick axe), *elaanku* (crowbar or a pointed iron rod for digging), *mazhu* (axe), *kari* (the blade of plough), etc., are manufactured by the blacksmiths. The villagers commonly use *katthi* for cutting vegetables, meat, etc. *Vettukatthi* is used for chopping or cutting and/or peeling big or hard items such as coconut, wood, etc. Earlier blacksmithy was an exclusive occupation of the caste Karuvan. Today, some others are also engaged in fabricating some of the iron implements. With the introduction of electric welding and lathe workshops, other castes and communities are also engaged in fabricating iron tools, gates, and iron grills.

Earlier, the Karuvan, the blacksmiths, used to make and supply various kinds of iron tools and equipment to almost all castes and communities but at present they do not supply these items moving from household to household. They supply the finished products or goods to the merchants in the urban centres and people buy them from the shops. The Viswakarma (Tamil Thattan) are the goldsmiths and their service is inevitable for all castes and communities. They are an in-migrant community. The Viswakarma (Kallan) provide mortar and grinding stones, which is indispensable for all households.

Household-to-household Supply of Goods or Door-to-door Selling

The caste Pandaran used to sell *pappadam,* a crispy food item, from household to household. But, in the changed situation they supply *pappadam* to the grocery shops within and outside the village. That is the traditional direct selling practice has come to an end with the advent of daily markets and shops within and outside the village.

The traditional door-to-door selling, or household-to-household supply or selling of goods was common in the villages up to 1980s. But with urbanisation, many more shops have been opened in the villages, and people have started buying them from the shops other than from the traditional suppliers who also produced them. The very change has become manifest in the interrelations of the castes and communities. Many items can be bought from the shops, and in such cases people do not have to go to the producers. In some cases where the service of people is inevitable, for example people cannot construct a house without the manual labour and skill of a carpenter and a mason, only in such circumstances the people rely on the service of the traditional as well as non-traditional workers. The "consumer culture" of the people has persuaded them to approach the jewellery shops in the town rather than going to the traditional goldsmith or the other caste goldworkers.

Many of the caste groups had enormous opportunities for interaction with the other caste groups. For example, the Kalarikurup, Viswakarma (Tamil Thattan), Viswakarma (Kallan), Marasari, Kallasari, Musari, Thattan, Karuvan, and Pandaran had direct contacts even in the earlier times. Since crucial change has taken place in the pattern of interaction in one way or other, all castes are now interacting each other.

Traditional Astrologer

The Kalarikurup, the traditional astrologers, of the village have no critical change as far as the service is concerned. Almost all castes and communities approach the Kalarikurup to know the auspicious day or time for conducting marriages, and other religious rituals, and for preparing horoscope of the newborn child. In the village the members of the caste Kalarikurup are permitted to visit the households of upper castes as well as lower castes in connection with their traditional service.

Inter-relations of castes and/or communities within a culture area are strong, but outside the culture area it is not so strong. The frequency of interactions with the people of this area, on the basis of caste and community is very limited, whereas the frequency of inter-relations and interactions in terms of commercial activities is more today. "The division of labour enjoyed by caste led to cooperation between neighbouring villages. Every village does not have every essential caste–in fact, it is frequently found that a Barber in village-A also serves B and C, and a Washerman in village-C also serves A and B, and so on. This is strikingly seen in Kerala where dispersed villages are the rule, and an artisan family has the rights of service (*avakasam*) in several neighbouring villages. The circles of villages served by each of the artisans in a village overlap only to a limited extent" (Srinivas, 1962:78). But, the recent facilities of conveyance have augmented the interaction of the traditional astrologers across various villages.

The Scheduled Castes

There are four Scheduled Castes in the village namely, the Perumannan, the Vettuvan, the Pulaya and the Paraya, and their social status is different from one another. The Perumannan had an inevitable role in the village. The female members of this caste group were washerwomen and they had to provide *maattu*, a clean cloth to the upper caste people and even for the Nambutiris. The acceptance of *maattu* has discontinued by the 1950s; however, some of the womenfolk were continuing their traditional occupation till 1980s. At present, almost all have stopped their traditional occupation because the new generations are more attracted to various other jobs than their traditional occupation. A number of them were traditional ayurvedic practitioners and have been enjoying great acceptance in the village as the traditional physicians. Some of them had shops where they practiced and dispensed herbal medicines. At present, this tradition has almost declined and the new generation is attracted to various occupations and their traditional interaction pattern has considerably changed. Earlier, it was based on their traditional service, but today interaction is in terms of non-traditional aspects. More over, when the teaching and learning of ayurveda shifted to colleges, the traditional people could not maintain a lot of new formalities of the current academic exercises. This has also paved the way for the withdrawal of the people from their traditional occupation.

The Vettuvan belonging to the Scheduled Castes and they are often mistaken as Pulayas, who were the agrestic serfs of Kerala. Some of the Vettuvans were agricultural labourers and some were the coconut pluckers. The Vettuvan claim that they are superior to the Pulayas. In point of caste restrictions, certainly the Vettuvan enjoyed better circumstances, and they had better daily contact with the higher classes in the ordinary concerns of life that afforded them greater facilities for increased knowledge and civilisation than the Pulayas and the Parayas. Besides, in this village, the condition of the Vettuvans and the Pulayas are more or less the same. Both of them are employed in agricultural labour and fencing.

Earlier, the Parayas used to approach their Nayar landlord or the Nambutiris from whom they received *punyaham* (holi water) and some milk, which had to be sprinkled on the woman and her newly born child after the 10th day of delivery. Only one or two male members used to visit the Nambutiri or the Nayar landlord.

The Parayas make baskets and winnowing pan and their service is inevitable for all castes and communities in the village. The Parayas was an untouchable caste that had a lower social status than that of the Pulayas. The Parayas were treated as the lowest of low castes. Earlier, they were not allowed to walk through the vicinity of houses of the upper castes. At present, some buy bamboo products from the Parayas. They freely interact with the other castes.

A greater part of the agricultural and other manual labour was done by the Pulayas. They never possessed any kind of property earlier. It was only after Independence (1947) and after the Land Reforms (1963 and 1969), they have got rehabilitated to the present set up. The earlier life and culture of the Pulayas is a typical example for the Master-Slave relationships of the feudal period.

When the Pulaya folk went for work in the paddy fields of the landlords, the Pulaya received food in the form of gruel. They had to make small pits on the ground and insert a piece of plantain leaf in the pit into which the housemaids of the master would serve food and return. The Pulaya was to remain aloof till then. Before the Pulaya member approached to eat and drink gruel, sometimes crows might have eaten some food from the pit. In this way they were kept extremely aloof from the life of the higher castes.

Social Interaction and Proximal Distance

Earlier, that is in the first quarter of the 20th century, the Pulayas had to keep a distance of 64 feet from the Nambutiris and 30 feet from the Nayars. If a Nambutiri felt that he was not 64 feet away from a Pulaya, the Nambutiri used to order the Nayar to measure the distance with a yard stick and if the distance was at least one or two feet less than 64, then the Nambutiri had to take a symbolic bath for purification. Besides, as a punishment the Pulaya would get a lot of thrashing on his back, usually with a long stick.

Though slavery was abolished in 1853 the slaves were in every way dependent on their former masters (Verghese, 1986:25). Many informants belonging to the Pulaya and Vettuvan remember that even after Independence they were attached to their masters and they could not sever the tie of the master-slave relationship easily. The Pulayas mostly mingle with the lower castes, yet, they observe strict policies, like, that they should not take food from a Paraya house and should not work for a lower caste. All these aspects have already become matters of the past.

The proximal distance also has to be maintained by the Vettuvan and the Parayas of the village. The Perumannan have received an incomparable acceptance, than other Scheduled Castes, by the Nambutiris because of the social functions like *maattu*, a clean loincloth supplied by the Perumannan woman in order to clean up pollution after birth, death, menstruation, etc.

The lower castes generally mingle with the lower castes. The Harijan colonies or the Scheduled Caste colonies developed by the various Governments of the post-independence period virtually have paved the way for cultural stagnation among the Scheduled Castes. Yet, many of the Scheduled Caste people do not manifest the grit and power to stand abreast with the "mainstream" of population. The very picture of the Scheduled Castes of the village show the nuances of cultural stagnation, despite the fact that the educated and urban life loving Scheduled Castes could come out of all the fetters of their traditional culture.

The abolition of slavery (1853), Vaikom Satyagraha (1924), Guruvayur Satyagraha (1931-32) Temple Entry (1947), Land Reforms (Kerala Agrarian Relations Act (1960), Kerala Land Reforms Act (1963), Kerala Land Reforms Act (1969)), education, the Marxist Party's teachings, the efforts of various caste leaders, the acts and measures taken by the State Government, etc., were some of the major factors, which helped the Scheduled Castes in improving their standards of life, and progress in the present socio-cultural spheres and eliminate a number of age-old customs. As a part of maintaining social equality, a number of activities were launched by the Government as well as some of the caste associations. Aiyappan (1992:40) says that, "In Kerala, after 1947, the Harijan Welfare Department persuaded ex-serf women to give up their bead necklaces and wear ornaments, if they could, of the patterns used by non-serf working class women. This campaign has more or less succeeded and in the plains of Kerala, women of the former serf castes are not distinguishable by their ornaments or dress".

The Christians and the Muslims

The Muslims and the Christians have become the part of the population. They have no traditional occupations as the caste groups possess; nevertheless, most of them are traders and agriculturists. They interact with all castes and communities with regard to their business and agriculture. Earlier, the Christians could go to the front yard of a Nambutiri *illam* (house), whereas the Ezhavas or the Scheduled Caste men could not go to such a place.

In-migrant Caste Groups and their Interaction

In-migration refers to movement into a particular area (Bhende & Kanitkar 1996: 303). The term is used to refer to the movement within a country. As far as the present context is concerned, it refers to the linguistic area of Malayalam speakers in general and the village in particular. There are many in-migrant caste groups in the village and they have not received a strong hold in the local caste hierarchy for a long time. The Embrantiri (Kannada Brahmins), Pattar (Tamil Brahmins),

Ezhuthachan, Nadar (Hindu), Viswakarma (Tamil Thattan), Viswakarma (Kallan), and the Kudumbi are some of them. The exact period of in-migration is not known. Of course, it is not relevant to the present analysis. However, the interaction pattern of the people is obviously relevant, as they have become the part and parcel of the village community. The Tamil Brahmins of the village are not at all engaged in their traditional pooja, whereas the Kannada Brahmins still perform their traditional service in some temples. The Ezhuthachan are positioned just below the higher castes and above the Ezhavas. As some of the Ezhuthachan are engaged in agriculture, they have had to interact with almost all categories of people in the village. The Kudumbi is in-migrated from the State of Goa, and their present traditional occupation is making rice flake. Some of them still continue their traditional occupations and interact with various castes and communities.

Modern Elements of Change

Change in occupations due to occupational diversification, has rightly influenced the interaction pattern within the village. Many of the earlier inter-caste relations have become non-existent now. As a result, a new pattern has emerged and the concept of inter-caste relation itself has vanished considerably.

Among almost all castes and communities, the intra and inter-interaction between members of a family and outside are different. Usually when a member belonging to a family meets a member of the other family, the behaviour varies from a kind of strangeness, familiarity, respect, politeness, friendliness, normal talk and even to gossiping.

The sudden change of pace of the development of the people is mainly due to the impact of the goldwork. Earlier, industrialisation like the advent of timber industries, tile factories, and the ayurveda industry (production and distribution of medicine) did not make a drastic change in the village.

It is quite obvious that the present development is only because of the change of concept of the people from purity and pollution to economic gains and better life styles. The traditional caste occupations have declined, and its significance has shifted from the dignity of occupation to economic gain. The "work culture" of the people too has radically transformed.

Though there are great changes in the interaction pattern of the people, there is yet no sign of the decline of caste system. The traditional caste-based occupation and service relations have taken a new direction. Naturally, some services have also discontinued along with the transformation that has taken place during the last fifty years.

Although the consciousness of the concept 'caste' is not strong among the members of the society, particularly in the social interaction, the traditional religious beliefs and practices still remain strong.

A crucial change has happened in the realm of traditional occupations of various castes groups in the village, and this has exerted obvious change in the pattern of inter-group interaction. A significant observation is that people interact with each other with some obvious purposes. Therefore, when the purposes change, the pattern of interaction also changes. For example, when people purchase various goods and/or commodities from the shops, the villagers themselves gradually modify or discourage some of the traditional relations with the other castes. The villagers rarely approach a weaver or a goldsmith or a blacksmith because now they find it easy to buy such items from the shops where they are available; this in turn modifies the traditional interaction pattern.

There are different categories of occupations including services and duties, which have disproportionate demand. Some occupations have higher demand and others have lesser demand. Based on the degree of demand, occupations have undergone modifications; some of them have disappeared. The services like carpentry, masonry, etc., retain the characteristic of on site services. In such circumstances, the Carpenter and the Mason will have to go to the premises of other caste people for rendering their services. Thus the traditional pattern is being maintained. At the time of extensive changes, people do not want to wait. For instance, they prefer to go to a jewellery shop for buying ornaments rather than giving an order to the local goldsmith. In former days, people had to place an order and wait for days and weeks for the finished jewellery.

At present, in the village, the castes like Pattar, Warriar, Nayar, Menon, Pillai, Kartha, Nadar, Viswakarma-Kallan, Kudumbi, and Paraya have absolutely abandoned their traditional occupations. Apart from this, the people themselves have started discarding traditional occupations due to low level of income or due to low status or due to change in social values. For instance, the Viswakarma-Kallan, Nadar, Kudumbi, and Paraya have stopped their occupation, since it is not income generating. The Perumannan women have abandoned their traditional occupation due to inferior status. At the same time, the Veluthedath Nayars continue their traditional occupation–washing the clothes of the higher castes like Nambutiri, Warriar, etc. And the Nayars have withdrawn their service due to change in values attached to their traditional service.

The functional role of castes and communities is being transformed to new directions with the changes in the socio-cultural values in general and the occupational realm in particular. Some services have lost their significance, for example, the palanquin bearing, oil pressing, etc. Some occupations such as goldwork and other industrial labour have become more popular due to their high income generating nature or due to monetary benefits. We can analyse the levels of change of each caste and community.

Table 1
Percentages of the Traditional and Modern Occupations of Castes

Sl. No.	*Caste (Sub castes are included with the castes) *The subcastes and titles are included in the same caste.*	*Percentage of Traditional Occupation*	*Percentage of Modern Occupation*
1.	Nambutiri	25	75
2.	Embrantiri	57	43
3.	Pattar	0	100
4.	Nambisan	25	75
5.	Warriar	0	100
6.	Marar	40	60
7.	Nayar*	0	100
8.	Veluthedath Nayar	18	82
9.	Velakkithala Nayar	60	40
10.	Ezhuthachan	26	74
11.	Ezhava	0.8	99.2
12.	Ezhavathi	50	50
13.	Nadar (Hindu)	0	100
14.	Kalarikurup	6	94
15.	Viswakarma (Tamil Thattan)	100	0
16.	Viswakarma (Kallan)	0	100
17.	Marasari	70	30
18.	Kallasari	53	47
19.	Musari	33	67
20.	Thattan	53	47
21.	Karuvan	30	70
22.	Pandaran	25	75
23.	Kudumbi	0	100
24.	Perumannan	4.5	95.5
25.	Vettuvan	50	50
26.	Pulaya	54	46
27.	Paraya	0	100

Table 2
Descending Percentages of the Traditional Occupations of Castes

Sl. No.	Castes	% Traditional Occupation
1.	Viswakarma (Tamil Thattan)	100
2.	Marasari	70
3.	Velakkithala Nayar	60
4.	Embrantiri	57
5.	Pulaya	54
6.	Kallasari	53
7.	Thattan	53
8.	Ezhavathi	50
9.	Vettuvan	50
10.	Marar	40
11.	Musari	33
12.	Karuvan	30
13.	Ezhuthachan	26
14.	Nambutiri	25
15.	Nambisan	25
16.	Pandaran	25
17.	Veluthedath Nayar	18
18.	Kalarikurup	6
19.	Perumannan	4.5
20.	Ezhava	0.8
21.	Pattar	0
22.	Warriar	0
23.	Nayar	0
24.	Nadar	0
25.	Viswakarma (Kallan)	0
26.	Paraya	0
27.	Kudumbi	0

Table 2 provides the descending percentage of traditional occupations of people belonging to different castes, and Table 3 shows the percentage of the modern occupations of the people belonging to the respective castes.

An economic aspect of the traditional occupations is also important because people continue their occupations in order to meet their livelihood. In general, people have abandoned some of their traditional occupations due to two major reasons; one, less income, two, inferior social status.

Table 3
Descending Percentages of the Modern Occupations of Castes

Sl. No	*Castes*	*% Modern Occupations*
1.	Pattar	100
2.	Warriar	100
3.	Nayar	100
4.	Nadar	100
5.	Viswakarma (Kallan)	100
6.	Paraya	100
7.	Kudumbi	100
8.	Ezhava	99.2
9.	Perumannan	95.5
10.	Kalarikurup	94
11.	Veluthedath Nayar	82
12.	Nambutiri	75
13.	Nambisan	75
14.	Pandaran	75
15.	Ezhuthachan	74
16.	Karuvan	70
17.	Musari	67
18.	Marar	60
19.	Ezhavathi	50
20.	Vottuvan	50
21.	Kallasari	47
22.	Thattan	47
23.	Pulaya	46
24.	Embrantiri	43
25.	Velakkithala Nayar	40
26.	Marasari	30
27.	Viswakarma (Tamil Thattan)	0

The economic aspect has greater significance as the people are doing all services and duties for a livelihood. Once the economic aspect of the occupations declines, people move onto other occupations for higher wages and thereby they achieve better means of livelihood. Changes in occupation and services have not changed the structure of the caste system. Despite, changes in the occupations and interaction pattern, the people continue endogamy and religious practices without much change.

The change in the pattern of interaction is due to the change in the overall socio-cultural change. Therefore, this change in the interaction is quite significant. Occupational diversification and occupational shift from the traditional occupations to the modern occupations are the causative factors for the present pattern of change in the inter-caste and inter-community proximal behaviours.

According to Radcliffe-Brown (1976: 190), 'culture' denotes not any concrete reality but an abstraction; whereas, the term 'social structure' denotes the network of actually existing relations, and it is not an abstraction. In my opinion the pattern of socio-cultural change is an abstraction developed from the change that have taken place in the village for the last few decades. And it is based on the actually existing relations without which it is impossible to make abstractions or conceptualizations and theory building. Therefore, reality and abstraction are the two different expressions of the same phenomenon. The conceptualization of facts is more significant in the present context.

The pattern of social interaction of the people of the village is similar to the one portrayed by Radcliffe-Brown (1976:190). Nevertheless, the above elucidation is not substantial to depict the present pattern of socio-cultural change of the heterogeneous population of the village, and the process and pattern of interaction is provided in the chapter-'Pecuniarisation–A New Theory of Social Change in India'.

The structural functional theory is not completely anachronistic as it is useful for explaining the general aspects of interaction of the people of the rural areas or villages. Social interaction is an important aspect of study as it is inevitable for the understanding of the structure of a multi-caste village. Different scholars have interpreted social structure in different ways. Radcliffe-Brown and Levi-Strauss kept their idea differently. When Radcliffe-Brown used actually existing relations for the construction or explanation of social structure, Levi-Strauss argued that the actually existing relations have nothing to do with the model making. He finds it as a raw material for the construction of a structural model. For the present study, both these conceptual and theoretical models of Radcliffe-Brown and Levi-Strauss have been employed to portray the *major pattern of interactions of various castes and communities*.

For Levi-Strauss (1963: 279) the term social structure has nothing to do with empirical reality but with models which are built up after it. He has differentiated the two concepts, namely, *social structure* and *social relations*. Social relations consist of the raw materials out of which the models making up the social structure are built, while social structure can be reduced to the ensemble of the social relations to be described in a given society.

As far as the caste and community interaction of this village is concerned, earlier almost all services and duties were provided exclusively through the caste lines, and the very model or pattern of traditional caste interaction provided the First Model (Early Model) - "*The Relations based on More Traditional Occupations and Less Modern Occupations*" and the Second Model (Contemporary Model) is based on "*The traditional and the modern occupational relations of the people of the village*".

It is important that, at present, only 25.4 per cent of the *households perpetuate their traditional occupation* in the traditional manner, whereas 74.6 per cent of the *households* have *abandoned their traditional occupation and services*. These figures point out the pattern of change

Graphics 1
Social Relations and Social Structure

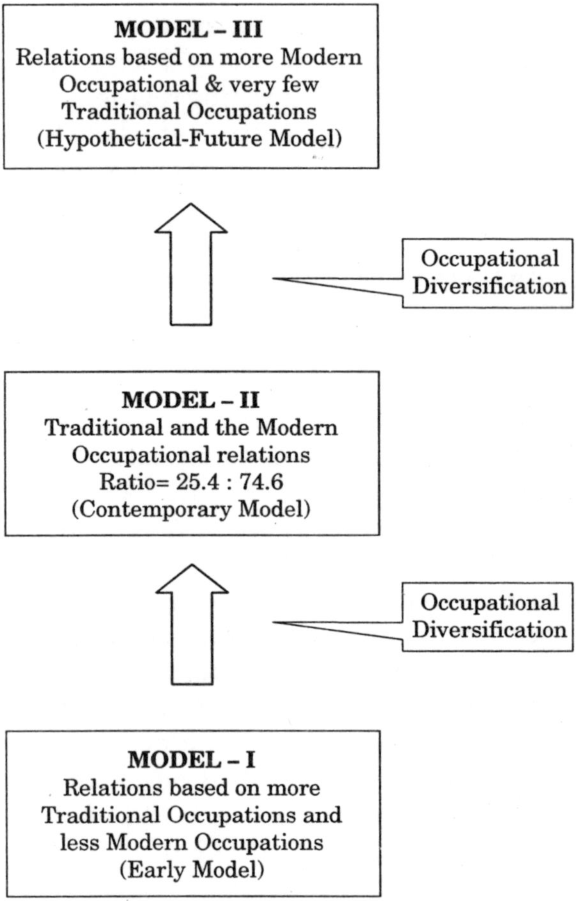

occurred within a village, and it has in turn altered the very traditional mode of social interaction and stipulated the contemporary social structure.

When we attempt to reduce all social life to theories or general statements about the nature of society, which allow prediction, and keeping this view in mind, we can develop a possible model (Model – III), which provides a critical picture of change in the interaction pattern. That is, in the future, most of the traditional occupations might disappear. Nevertheless, some of the traditional services and occupations appertain to the very religious beliefs will linger. Therefore, social interaction would not absolutely be based on modern occupations and services in the village communities. This is applicable not only to Kerala but also to the whole country. The "social relations" and "social structure" of the village can be diachronically and diagrammatically shown as follows.

The structural functional theory of Radcliffe-Brown and the structural theory of Levi-Strauss are helpful to provide the general principle of the social interaction and its model making. Nevertheless, those concepts are not substantial to provide the very particular characteristic of the socio-cultural change that is taking place in the multi-caste villages. Social and cultural interaction patterns of various people are quite dynamic and integrated. The notion of each and every element of culture juxtaposes the latent and manifest elements of social process and structure.

5

PECUNIARISATION—A NEW THEORY OF SOCIAL CHANGE IN INDIA

This chapter provides an overall picture of socio-cultural change of the village with particular emphasis on the changes due to occupational diversification and occupational change. An analysis of the present problem and its theoretical explanations are also made in this chapter.

Different scholars have used the terms "social" and "cultural" differently. Harris (1983: 6) says, "Some sociologists and anthropologists employ the term "social" to refer to the relationships among the groups within a society. For these social scientists, culture consists of the life ways of the members of a society apart from the society's group structure". For Harris (ibid.) a society is a group of people who share a common habitat and who are dependent on one another for their survival and well-being.

The term "cultural" is the adjective of the term "culture" and it has been defined by a number of anthropologists and yet inquires for comprehensive definitions extended up to the words of Tylor. In the words of Tylor (1871) culture is "that complex whole which includes knowledge, belief, art, morals, law, custom, and any other capabilities and habits acquired by man as a member of society." Gerald Weiss (1969) (quoted in Mann 1984: 173) included organizational network of inter-relationships and interactions (social organization) and ideas under culture. Another definition says, "[All the] historically created designs for living, explicit and implicit, rational, irrational, and nonrational, which exist at any given time as potential guides for the behavior of man" (Kluckhohn and Kelly 1949) (quoted in Keesing 1981:68).

In essence, culture is a complex whole and it has a network of inter-relations, and it is a continuity of historically created design, which has dynamic structure(s) and its paradigm based on a qualitative and quantitative inquiry is worked out here in the present book.

Occupational Diversification and Socio-Cultural Change

New occupational opportunities have been the basis of the present change. It was in the 1960s the first industry came up in the village, and that was a timber industry. Later on two small-scale industries of the same kind were established. But the period between 1980 to 1990 was a time of industrial growth in this area, which is still continuing. There are three metal workshops, and a hollow brick manufacturing unit, and these industries are manufacturing materials for construction of houses and buildings. There are two quarries where they make raw materials for the construction of roads, houses, buildings, etc. These ventures provide new vocational opportunities for the people of this traditional village.

In general, most of the industries are small-scale units using indigenous as well as modern technology. These industries provide more or less stable labour supply throughout the year. It has helped to reduce unemployment among the villagers considerably. When the occupational scene got diversified, many caste people gave up their traditional occupation and moved to new jobs. This is only one phase of the change of the village. The planned change is positioned on the other side.

After Independence, the Government of India realised the importance of rural development and launched extensive plans and programmes, which brought about a series of changes in the village communities. For instance, "The Community Development Programme was launched by the Government of India, on 2nd October, 1952 with a view to achieving the total transformation of the Indian social order from the folk to the secular" (Ainapur 1986: 137). Besides this, a number of development and welfare measures have been initiated in order to bring the rural masses to the mainstream of national development. The initiation of various welfare measures in the field of education, health, sanitation, family planning, housing and special welfare programmes for the Weaker Sections including women, Scheduled Castes, etc., made it possible to improve the living standards of the rural masses.

All these planned programmes were directly and indirectly helping to diversify the occupational scene considerably. The diversification of occupations has strengthened the inter-caste, inter-village, village-town, and national and international relations. The communication skill of the people living in different socio-cultural levels also has improved. These changes are progressively reflecting on the life-style of the people in a continuous process. With the advent of industrialisation, the people could find new job opportunities in different areas other than their traditional caste bound occupations. This ultimately exposed the traditional vocational groups to new areas of life and culture. Expansion of economy, improvement of technology, expansion of transportation and communication facilities, introduction of modern educational system, etc., reached the villages of India. Communication and mass media have made a considerable progress along with the facilities of transport and conveyance.

From the last four to five decades or with the commencement of industrialisation, modernisation, education, etc., the vocational scene has considerably changed and diversified. The new educational set up opened up many employment opportunities throughout the country and a good number of them have achieved good education and migrated from the village for white-collar jobs in the public and private sectors in other States of India as well as overseas.

A major change related to the present development is that people enjoy more freedom to select occupations according to their own interests, whereas in the traditional set up there was no freedom. Earlier, "generally a caste or a group of allied castes considered some of the calling as its hereditary occupation, to abandon which in pursuit of another, though it might be more lucrative, was thought not to be right" (Ghurye 1986:15). At present, an agricultural labour can go to a tile factory or a timber industry for finding a job for his livelihood. But, the only thing is that he/she should be competent to do the assigned works of the respective industries. This change has, virtually, been initiated from the onset of industrialisation. Nevertheless, large-scale industrialisation has not yet taken place. Only small industries have come up till date.

The advent of the Ayurveda medicine preparing industry in the adjacent village has helped a number of villagers to get various jobs in the industry and its impact can also be observed in the life and culture of the villagers. It is quite significant that a number of Nayar families have become self reliant only due to the permanent jobs provided by the industry. The tile factories, another major sector, which flourished during the 1980s, attracted a number of agricultural labourers to the industry. Later,

Figure 1
Growth of the Village Economy Since Independence

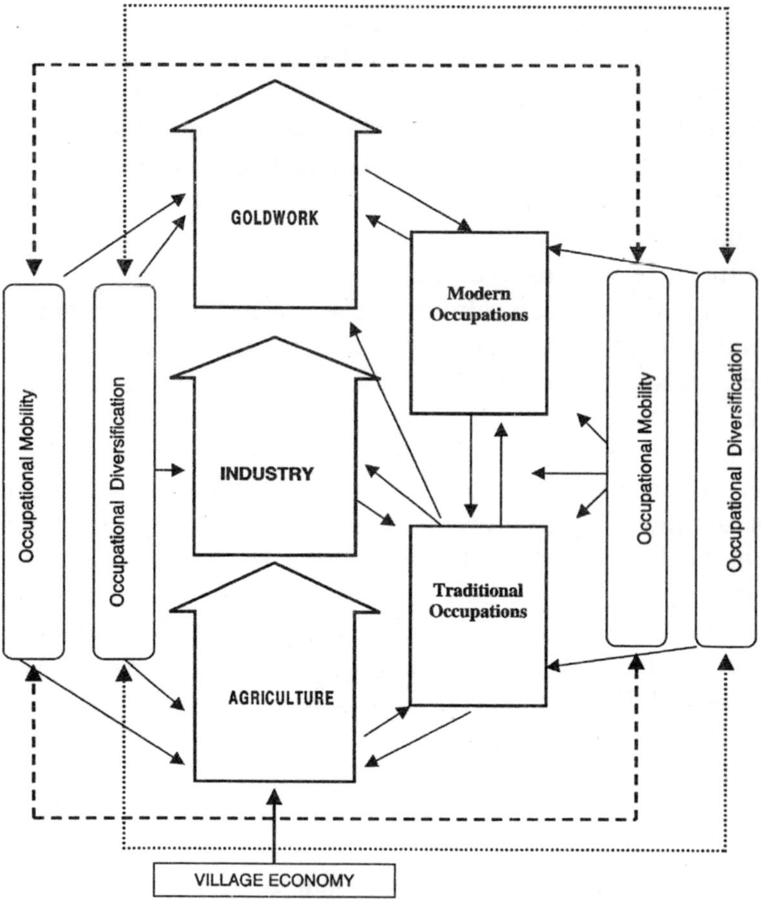

by 1995s, this industry faced tremendous problems and a number of tile factories have been closed due to lack of raw materials and demand for tiles. That is, the industries changed the occupations of the people from the agriculture to industrial labourers, and later the industries have neglected the labourers.

The decline of agriculture also has happened with the labourer scarcity and industries. Some of the industrial labourers were able to find avenues in other villages and some of them confined to their households. This was the period of the growth of the goldwork in the village. Some of the agricultural and industrial labourers, particularly those category of fathers and mothers of the young goldworkers, confined to their homesteads.

Basically, the village economy has transformed from agriculture to industry and then further changed to goldsmithy. Radical changes took place in these three spheres during the last five decades. The changes in the subsistence pattern, and the changes in the agricultural practices, and the changes in the pattern of occupational mobility are some of the major aspects of the village economy. Agriculture was the mainstay of the village economy up to the 1970s. The second phase, that is the growth of the industry, is only a post Independence phenomenon as far as the village is concerned. The third phase is the one and the only phase, which has been the pivotal aspect of change of the village. Therefore, adequate emphasis has been provided for this aspect throughout the presentation and discussion.

Changes in the Agricultural Sector

Traditionally, when monsoon comes in the May–June, the farmers prepare seed beds and sow paddy in them and after 28 or 30 days they are transplanted in the ploughed field. In the present day, mechanisation has also been adopted in agricultural practices like the use of power tillers and tractors for the preparation of the field, replacing the ancient plough. Now, the use of plough and cattle has become a rare sight in the village.

A man with a pair of cattle and plough said that it was too difficult to maintain a pair of cattle only for the two season's work. He added that as the income from cultivation is meagre, it is difficult even to feed the cattle; consequently, the ploughmen cannot maintain cattle for this purpose alone. When mechanisation is adopted, people find it easy to get their agricultural land ready with minimum labour and time. The mechanisation in agricultural sector is an obvious reflection of the overall modernisation of the society. Although there has been amelioration as a part of the developments, non-availability of agricultural labourers has become a serious problem presently.

As far as the agricultural practice of this village is concerned, apart from the occupational mobility and industrialisation there are other factors for the devastation of agricultural system such as the increased prices for fertilisers, pesticides and wages. This shows that the expenditure towards agricultural operation is more than the yield. All these together compelled them to abandon agriculture to some extent.

By and large, the cost of dry land is rising because of industrialisation, occupational shift and increase in the buying power of the people. The medium families are approaching the wetland owners, particularly those who discontinued cultivation, because the price of wetland is less than the dry land, and finally these agricultural lands are being converted into non-cultivating land.

It is so significant that a good number of agricultural labourers have given up their agricultural labour and moved onto industrial sectors and become industrial labourers today. The absorption of the agricultural labourers to the industrial sector has considerably devastated the agricultural system of this area. Many acres of wetland are left fallow and are being used for non-agricultural purposes. In some places, wetland is left as grazing land or used for coconut cultivation. Apart from this people have started constructing houses in the paddy fields, since the cost of wetland is lower than that of dry land.

The fertile soil of the paddy fields is being used for manufacturing bricks. Thus, the paddy fields are becoming uncultivable land with large pits and ditches. Among the modes of conversion of agricultural land to other purposes, the use of paddy fields for brick manufacturing, erecting houses, and for coconut cultivation are the common practices which not only break the backbone of cultivation but also disturbs the ecological balance.

As far as the cultural change is concerned, the culture is active and the environmental determinism is worthless. "Today the theme of environmental determinism has been largely replaced by the emergence of man-environmental models that assign environment a "limiting" but uncreative role or that recognize complex mutual interaction" (Hardestry 1977: 3). According to Kaplan and Manners (1972:79) (quoted in Hardestry 1977: 9) the concept of reciprocal causality has two ideas and [1] the idea that neither environment nor culture is a "given" but that each is defined in terms of the other, and [2] the idea that environment plays an *active*, not a limiting or selective, role in human affairs. At the same time it must be kept in mind that the relative influence of environment and culture in a feedback relationship is not equal. Now, people are adopting new strategies to exploit cultivable land. That is, culture is playing a more active role at least in the devastation of agricultural practice in this village.

At present, this village has become the culture area where the jewellery work is flourishing. The spread of goldwork in this village is affecting agriculture. It is because majority of the people that have entered into goldwork is from the Backward and Scheduled Castes, and many of them, particularly the older generation, had been agriculturists and agricultural labourers. In addition, the people of the village feel that agriculture labour has an inferior status, since it is not income generating. Thus, everyday, the number of people involved in agriculture labour is decreasing, whereas the number of people attracted towards industries and other vocations is increasing. Earlier, agriculture was the mainstay of the village economy. It is not only the fact that there were traditional agricultural labourers, but also that many people belonging to Backward Caste were also engaged in agricultural activities.

At present, the agricultural labourers constitute 11 per cent of the population. There are 23 per cent industrial labourers and 29 per cent goldworkers. This means that the percentage of non-agricultural labourers is 52. In essence, the goldwork, industrial and other occupational sectors dislodged the agricultural sector from its significant position. It could also be asserted that all other sectors show the behaviour of industries, whereas the agricultural sector has not developed sufficiently. The caste-bound traditional society is, virtually, loosing its traditional roles.

Changes in the Traditional Occupations

Significant changes can be observed now in the field of traditional occupations. A great change has happened in the perception of traditional occupation or caste-based occupation, as a result of which many people have adopted the occupations of other castes mainly due to monetary benefits. Goldwork, carpentry, and masonry are some of the major occupations that have been adopted by other castes. Of these, goldwork has attained utmost importance due to its high monetary returns. As a part of this change, a carpenter can engage himself in making gold ornaments. An Ezhava also can engage either in goldwork or in carpentry. There are many such instances in this village since a few decades. There is neither restriction nor is it considered as a disgraceful activity in adopting the vocation of a lower caste. The main emphasis is on money and/or sufficient income for subsistence.

When the traditional occupation, particularly the goldwork, got an effective acceptance amongst the other caste members, it also got modified with mechanisation. Mechanisation in place of use of some peculiar tools like pincers, pliars, small cutting tools, etc., has improved the quality and artistic beauty of the finished products.

Now a number of modern motorised tools are used. This mechanisation has greatly helped the other caste members to master the work. Different types of machines are used for making different kinds of ornaments.

Apart from mechanisation, job specialisation also has come into existence. That is to say, some make the ornaments, others polish it, and other experts give final touches to the ornaments. But among the traditional workers, there was no such specialisation, a worker knew all the areas of the work. This type of occupational shift has been identified in the contiguous villages and some other parts of the Thrissur district.

Changes in the Work-Culture of Traditional Sectors

The change in the work-culture has happened due to the increased opportunities in various sectors of production and distribution. Of course, the middlemen have their own advantage. The changes in the work-culture persuade the people to leave hard labour and accept or select easier jobs. The change in the work-culture and the change in the trading pattern of the goods produced are the major reasons for the growth of the industry.

In the goldwork, as there are no restrictions imposed, people could work at pleasure. It is advantageous because it helps them earn more money according to their aspirations provided that they find avenues for supplying the finished goods. For that they tour the other districts in Kerala and go even to other States, namely, Tamil Nadu and Karnataka.

It is very important that the goldwork must be done in a time-bound manner without which it is difficult to stick on to the job. It is because, if one does not supply the finished goods in time, the jewellery owner incurs heavy loss. The workers have to maintain punctuality besides having good skill in making various types of gold ornaments.

As there is no intra-village demand or market, the goldworkers of this village as well as adjacent villages go to various places all over Kerala and other places like Coimbatore, Chennai, etc., in Tamil Nadu, and Bangalore and Mangalore in Karnataka. The high risk involved in the goldwork further forces the owners to employ more number of workers within one residential gold-working unit itself, and the pattern has spread over the villages quickly.

The migratory character of the goldworkers paved the way for inter-village, inter-district, and inter-state opportunities of interaction. It provided them an opportunity for acculturation leading to socio-cultural change.

The working hours also increased beyond imagination. They work day and night to complete the work according to time. Some gold-working units have power generators in order to work during power cuts and/or failures. Apart from this, the new generation gold workers use a number of motorised machines to enhance the various levels of production.

The traditional goldsmiths find it difficult to compete with the other caste goldworkers now. The traditional goldsmiths were concentrating on the local areas or the home town, Thrissur. At the same time, as the number of other caste goldworkers keep increasing, the new goldworkers are forced to find market somewhere in the adjacent districts. This ultimately helped them to open a wider market zone for them.

Earlier goldsmithy was a traditional occupation solely of the goldsmiths, i.e., Thattan and Viswakarma, who had attained maximum acceptance among the villagers. Presently, a number of highly educated as well as less educated persons have come to this occupation, which completely modernised the job sector within the village.

When the younger generation started earning considerably from this economic activity, the older generation has been forced to confine to their homes. Most of the agricultural as well as tile factory labourers stick on to their household jobs, such as cooking food, and looking after their grand children. Nevertheless, there are some exceptional cases where the parental generation has not abandoned their earlier jobs, although their son(s) earn a lot.

Changes in the Amenities of Life

High income has provided better amenities of life that in turn has enhanced the pace of their life. A number of workers have become good businessmen too. They have subscribed to land telephones and mobile phones. At least a two-wheeler has become an inevitable means of transportation for them. Some of them have cars. Many of them have constructed good R.C.C. houses with modern facilities.

They provide good education to their children. Though there are two Malayalam medium schools within the village, some of their children are studying in English medium schools elsewhere paying high fees. Besides, there are a number of schools in the contiguous villages. English medium schools as a rule have their own vehicles for the transportation of students. These were possible only due to the steady growth of the gold industry within the village. Almost all the goldworkers studied only in the Malayalam medium schools within and in the adjacent villages. But, now they are in favour of English education, which may be because of the outside cultural contact.

A number of families virtually have forgotten their earlier difficulties for the primary as well as secondary needs. The youngsters have no time to roam here and there without any specific vocation as of the earlier time. Further, the awareness of the problems of the gold workers helps them to overcome a number of hurdles in the field of goldwork.

Like advantages, there are disadvantages too. Since a very large number of persons depend on gold industry for their livelihood, any change in the international and national market quickly affects their income. During the off-seasons when the price of gold comes down, small entrepreneurs become upset whereas the big businessmen succeed without much trouble.

It does not mean that all the goldworkers have flourished. Some of them have found it difficult to continue the goldwork and therefore gone to other jobs. Some of them have even ruined their life due to excessive loss as well as mismanagement of income. Further, it has been observed that the older generation did not enter into this occupation.

When we look into the new avenues of occupations of the people, we understand that generalisations become very difficult. For example, in terms of the occupations, only the youngsters are entering into goldwork, because it requires good eyesight, patience, and skills. But, those who are above 40 years are not showing interest in it; they are moving to the industrial sector. As far as the educational status of the goldworkers is concerned, most of them have only elementary education. But there are some graduates also in this profession.

Changes in the Caste Tag of Traditional Occupations

The caste tag of traditional occupations has not completely declined in many cases, whereas in other cases, caste tag exists only in the name of the occupation and caste tag has declined considerably. For example, the caste tag of the goldsmithy has almost vanished, and there is no other traditional occupation that has attained so much acceptance within the village within such a short period.

At present, goldwork has become a high income generating household industry. In the early stages of occupational mobility towards goldwork, most of the people were hesitant to speak about goldwork. At present, the youngsters have no such problems. More over, some of them could elevate their position from mere goldworkers to Jewellery shop owners outside the village, mainly in the urban places. The caste tag based occupations have declined to a minimum and in some cases it has completely disappeared. A few traditional occupations exist today due to economic reasons only.

"Today there are many areas of life which are becoming progressively caste-free" "(Beteille, 1965: 5). Occupational diversification has rightly helped the people to enter into a large number of occupations other than their traditional caste occupations. Presently, most of the traditional occupations have become caste-free occupations; for instance, goldwork, carpentry, etc. The occupational diversification has in turn helped to alter the caste-occupations to non-caste occupations. Moreover, the caste-free feeling developed among the people due to economic reasons has also helped to diversify the occupational sector.

Transition from ascribed status to a level of achieved status has become obvious at present, and it is due to the occupational diversification and the resultant change. The caste tag of the traditional occupations, particularly high income generating occupations has declined, which is a crucial change as far as the village community is concerned.

Earlier, the occupational shift within the caste occupations was extremely rare due to the caste feeling.

The spread of secular education and the awakening programmes of the Government of post Independent period have helped the people to behave differently. The social movements and the political movements also have paved the way for drastic change within the village.

Currently, the stature of the ascribed status is confined to some religious practices and the occupational sector has considerably got detached from the caste system. Some of the caste occupations have completely perished, and some of them are on the edge of disappearance. Many occupations have attained the dimension of modern entrepreneurship. In general, the occupational sector is no more a barrier for the achieved status. With the economic wealth and social uplift, people could achieve higher status in the village life. Therefore, today the modernized traditional occupations provide a higher social status to the people compared to the past.

It is very striking that the direction of change can be analysed by considering the age group analysis. According to which it is very conspicuous that what weighs with the younger generation of the society is the economic aspect of occupations rather than the social status. Social status was earlier considered to be superior with the occupations of the higher castes and inferior with the duties and services of the lower castes of the caste hierarchy. The traditional occupation of the goldsmiths was not a superior occupation even if they had to provide ornaments to the higher castes as well as to the gods and goddess and/or temples.

Changes in the Caste Identity

There is not much difference in the physical appearance of the people at present. The traditional dress pattern of the people has changed considerably, and recognising people on the basis of the dress pattern is quite difficult. The Nambutiris (Brahmins) continue their traditional dress while performing *pooja* in temples. They had changed their traditional dress pattern long ago. Lower castes and the higher caste people wear similar types of dress, and therefore, there is no difference, and it is difficult to identify castes and communities in terms of dress and appearance. However, the dress pattern of the aged Christian women and the dress pattern of the Muslim is quite different from others.

In-migrant Businessmen and Goldworkers and the Changes

The in-migration of "*Settus*" from the Maharashtra State to the village and the neighbouring villages is basically due to the growth of goldwork industry. The *Settus* have opened small shops within the village for purifying gold. There are no other people engaged in this vocation. All the goldworkers irrespective of caste and community approach the *Settus* for testing and/or purifying gold.

The arrival of goldsmiths from Kolkata is the latest phenomenon of this industry; however, there are no Bengali goldworkers in this village. They have settled in the adjacent villages as well as in the Thrissur town and provide service at low wages.

Advent of Goldwork by the Other Castes

During 1960s a member belonging to the Musari caste, the traditional braziers, learned goldwork and he started a shop in another village far away from the village. Later, it was during 1980 some members belonging to the Christian and Ezhava communities entered into goldwork. This decade virtually became a period of the occupational mobility towards goldwork, and the trend continues even now.

Although goldwork is a caste-based occupation, the overall changing environment in the village life has attracted some of the people, particularly the youngsters to this occupation and accordingly many members of the other castes initiated occupational mobility within the caste occupations. The traditional goldsmith castes namely the Thattan and the Tamil Viswakarma did not oppose the other castes adopting their traditional occupation.

Impact of Goldwork

Some of the goldworkers belonging to other castes have built new RCC houses during the last one decade (1990-2000). But, recently, some of them have sold their houses and land due to severe financial stress.

The use of various types of vehicles is increasing day by day in the village. Many youngsters among the other caste goldworkers have started using motorcycles and scooters, and which has become an indispensable thing among them. The use of cars is also not uncommon.

Some of the new goldworkers have invested their earnings in business related to goldwork, such as, dye work, tools selling shops, jewellery, etc. Some of them have opened dye works within the village. Jewellery shops and tools shops are opened in towns and other urban centres. There is no jewellery shop opened within the village.

The goldwork has become a major economic activity of the people of this village. When it captured a strong hold of the village economy, many people have confined absolutely to this vocation and their working hours extended from 13 to 16 hours a day, which is characteristic of the modern societies. They have adopted the use of power generators to avoid power cuts and power failures. Households of many goldworkers have started using power generators due to various reasons. The first reason is that they will have to provide the finished goods in time, otherwise they would lose opportunities as there is tough competition in this field. Secondly, in some households, a large numbers of workers are working under one non-traditional goldworker. In such circumstances, the employer buys power generators to avoid power failures, and this would help him to exploit the work of his employees effectively.

Most of the goldworkers find a work place in their own house. But in other cases they have built separate sheds or rooms near their houses exclusively for goldwork. Though their working hours and involvement in this vocation are rather high, the financial outcome is not commensurate with their work and this shows their strong relation with marketing and trade centres.

Goldwork has created various interaction patterns with the main workers and jewellery owners. The jewellery owners give enough gold biscuits to the workers who after the completion of the work return the finished ornaments to the jewelleries. But to obtain such a contact, one has to supply finished ornaments to the jewellery regularly thus establishing ones credibility.

Unemployment is a rare thing as far as the villagers are concerned. In fact, they find no time to attend to other works due to long working hours in gold work. At present, the economic efficiency of the traditional goldworkers is far below the non-traditional goldworkers.

People have more problems in finding a Govt. job or any other good job in private sectors. It is lack of high educational qualifications, which compels them to enter in goldwork. Since goldwork has the style of a cottage industry, experience is not asked for when they turn to this vocation. Moreover, within a few months they learn the preliminary and within one or two years, they learn more from their masters about goldwork industry. This in turn gives them confidence to start gold working independently. The newly trained goldworker opts to sit in his house and starts producing gold ornaments. This is the reason for the spread of goldwork in the village.

Competition among the goldworkers is minimal because they find new avenues throughout South India to supply the finished products. But, the villagers mostly rely on the jewelleries in Kerala. Every week they supply the finished ornaments to these jewellery shops.

Earlier, the villagers used to approach the traditional goldworkers and the demands of the villagers were met from within the village. Therefore, the traditional goldworkers were not connected with urban centres or towns. But, when the number of gold workers belonging to other castes increased, the production has also increased irrespective of the demand of the villagers. As a result, the new gold workers started moving outside the village particularly to the urban centres and towns. This has in turn helped them to have outside exposure which has stimulated a change of the life style of the people of the traditional village.

At the moment, the occupational mobility to goldwork has attained a high momentum. In the early half of the last decade (1990 – 2000) the school going children were also attracted to this vocation because of the luxurious life of the goldworkers. By the end of the decade, this trend has reduced to a minimum due to the extreme competition developed in the field with the excessive occupational mobility in the goldwork.

Impact of Occupational Diversification

Various aspects of occupational diversification have already been delineated in the former part of this chapter; however, an attempt is made here to analyse the impact of occupational diversification. The impact of occupational diversification is an important area, as the very process has become the causative as well as crucial factor for the extensive and pervasive changes of the village community.

A comprehensive definition of occupational diversification has been provided in the former chapter, and it is defined as 'the introduction of new occupations into the existing occupational scene or existing occupations into emerging or novel social requirements'. The process of occupational diversification is also dealt with in the previous chapter.

The analysis of the cause-effect relationship of the changes in the already existing occupations, the traditional and/or caste-based occupations, and the commencement of the new and non-caste occupations provide an outline for the impact of occupational diversification.

In the contiguous decade of Independence, there were no major non-caste occupational sectors prevalent in this village. Nevertheless, the agricultural practice and activities were a major occupational sector as well as a major means of livelihood for the villagers.

There are 12 caste groups and a community engaged in the agricultural sector as agriculturists, agricultural labourers, agriculturists-cum-agricultural labourers, and agricultural labourers-cum-coolie. They are namely, Nambutiris, Nayar (Vellaima Sudra), Nayar (Sudra), Nayar (Pallichan), Ezhuthachan, Ezhava, Kalarikurup, Karuvan, Kudumbi, Vettuvan, Pulaya, Paraya, and Christian.

In the agricultural sector, the Nambutiri, Nayar (Sudra), and Nayar (Pallichan) own agricultural land and they continue to be agriculturists. The Ezhava, Ezhuthachan and the Christian have agricultural land and they continue to be agriculturists-cum-agricultural labourers. Nayar (Velllaima Sudra) and Kudumbi have agricultural land and they live as agriculturists, agricultural labourers and coolies. The Pattar, and the Warriar own agricultural land but no family members are engaged primarily in the agricultural practice. They relied completely on the traditional agricultural labourers for their cultivation.

In this village, there are 11 castes and communities having agricultural fields, they are the land-owning agriculturists of the village, and they cultivate paddy. The traditional agricultural labourers are working for these landowners. The caste Pulaya and Vettuvan are the traditional agricultural labourers-cum-coolie in this village. The Kalarikurup, Karuvan and the Paraya have become landless agricultural labourers. It is obvious that only the affluent families possess agricultural land. In most of the cases some of the family members are also found engaged in agricultural labour along with the hired labourers. But the land-less, non-traditional agricultural labourers' activity can be considered as the occupational shift of the non-traditional labourers to the area of work of the traditional labourers. Therefore, it can be seen that some members of the caste Kalarikurup, Karuvan, and Paraya have entered into the traditional occupation of the Pulayas and the Vettuvan.

Further, if we take the number of agricultural labourers, the castes and communities like Kalarikurup, Karuvan, Paraya, Kudumbi, Nayar (Vellaima Sudra), Ezhuthachan, and Christian are engaged as agricultural labourers. Thus, six castes and a community have adopted the traditional occupation of the traditional agricultural labourers and agricultural work has been seen as the first area, which has been transformed into the level of non-caste occupations in the village.

In essence, in the traditional occupational scene, agricultural sector provided more opportunities for villagers. Industrialisation stood in the second place in providing opportunities in the non-caste occupational sector. The occupations in the government and private sector were also rare in the village in the 1950s and 1960s. During this period, only a few people received non-caste occupations within the village.

It was with the advent of industrialisation in the village, that the people began to have non-caste occupations. When people were able to find occupations in timber industries, tile factories, etc., they experienced the advantages of such occupations without much seasonal fluctuation. The industries provided more or less stable labour intake throughout the year. Thus, it reduced unemployment among the villagers considerably. When the occupational scene got diversified, many people gave up their traditional occupations and moved to new jobs.

It is so significant that a good number of agricultural labourers gave up their agricultural labour and moved to industrial sectors and became industrial labourers. There were many reasons for this transition. The most important reason was that agriculture provided only seasonal labour opportunities, whereas the industries provided more or less stable labour supply throughout the year. In addition, the industrial labourers were receiving bonus, and cash advances during the festival seasons like Onam, Vishu, Christmas, etc., in addition to their wages. They were also brought into the provident fund scheme, which was an added benefit for the industrial labourers and all these attracted many agricultural labourers to the industries within and outside the village.

It was in the 1970s that people began to receive more occupations in the non-caste occupational sector such as industries and private companies, in and outside the village. The decade starting from 1980 was a little more assertive in facilitating non-caste occupations. However, the decade 1990 to 1999 was very tough and during this period, excessive industrialisation and excessive shift of traditional occupation to non-traditional occupation took place. The growth of industries in the village had both positive and negative impacts. So far industrialisation has provided many occupational opportunities for the villagers in the skilled as well as unskilled areas of occupations.

But, even then, industrialisation faced difficulties due to occupational shift towards some caste occupations, particularly to the money minting goldwork.

Due to economic uplift, the families that had entered into goldwork insisted that their parents, who were agricultural labourers, should not go out for agriculture labour. It was also because of the fact that the people considered agriculture labour less lucrative and inferior in status. Thus, the number of people engaged in agriculture labour diminished day by day whereas the number of people attracted towards industries rose.

The excessive growth of goldwork has invited commercial problems, as the jewellers could not sell the whole of their finished gold ornaments within the village, and as a result they had to visit other places in the State and even go to other States in India. These opportunities made them mingle with the rest of the people who had different cultures and living styles. Thus changes took place in their lifestyle. The change can be referred to as acculturation. Acculturation is the process of cultural change, which occurs when two people with different cultures come into long and intimate contact. According to Oswalt (1986: 329) "acculturation is the process whereby the members of one culture assume characteristics of another one following an extended period of contact between them".

Some of the traditional occupations were seasonal but the vocations in the industries were somewhat permanent. Permanent income helped the people to lead a better way of life, which in turn brought about strength for family life. This has resulted in the feeling of individuality among the people, and in course of time nuclear families have emerged.

"Consumer culture" was an after-effect of occupational diversification. When the occupational sector experienced more specialisations, the villagers could not produce everything they wanted, but had to purchase such items from the shops. Even before this people used to buy a lot of things from the shops. But, at present the fast moving life style of the people is the main factor leading to the consumer culture.

In the present day, only a few are perpetuating their traditional occupation. The youngsters have started new enterprises within the village, and this is reducing the caste feelings in the industrial and other work places, whereas in the Government sector the caste feelings and considerations still have a strong sway.

As a result of modernisation most of the caste groups have given up their traditional occupations. But some of them like the Goldsmiths, Carpenters, Astrologers, and Blacksmiths are obviously maintaining their traditional occupations only because they have great demand within and outside the village. At present the demand for their traditional occupations seems to be increasing steadily.

When we look into the levels of unemployment, it shows a low level, and it is precisely because of the occupational mobility. Among this unemployed minority, most of them are educated and are expecting jobs either in the governmental or private sector, according to their educational standards.

Impact of Occupational Diversification on Marriage

A number of scholars have defined marriage, and a few of them are given here to comprehend the denotations and connotations of marriage. In the words of Oswalt (1986: 122), "marriage is a socially approved union between two or more persons, usually of the opposite sex, who share mutual obligations; it involves living together, economic cooperation, and reproduction". "Marriage is the institutionalised and legitimate form of man and woman relationship based on sex. It is related with the procreation of children, their upbringing, descent and inheritance"

(Dubey 1955: 15). "Gough (1961) sees "marriage as being, in all times and places, a customary transaction that serves to establish the legitimacy of newborn children as acceptable members of society" (Keesing 1981:252). "Marriage may be defined as a publicly recognised and culturally sanctioned union between a male and a female, which is intended to be enduring, to give primary (but not necessarily exclusive) sexual rights in each other to the couple, and to fulfil further social functions." (Jha, 1994:39). Jha further added that "a limited number of ends, including child rearing, economic partnership between husband and wife, and the formation of alliances between kin groups, are characteristic of marriage in many societies." (ibid.). Marriage is based on the desire to perpetuate one's family line. In general, marriage is the basis for the formation of families; and the selection of spouse, the marriage ceremony, gifts and familial cooperation are significant aspects for the stability of marriage.

Occupational diversification has also become a factor for change in the socio-cultural side of marriages. As occupation is a means of livelihood for each person, the occupational diversification provides more opportunity for the people to achieve better means of livelihood according to their desires, at least upto some extent. Both these have helped the people to augment the socio-economic condition and amenities of life, which in turn has helped to improve the overall prospects of marriage except with regard to the caste/community and religious tags.

At present, most of the marriages are conducted after three or four mutual visits of the members and relatives of both the girls and boys. The groom and one or two friend and/or relatives visit the girl's house and the girl is introduced to them. This is commonly known as *pennukaanal*. After this, the relatives of the bride's family, if they wish to proceed with the proposal, visit the bridegroom's house. Later, the groom's relatives visit the bride's house for the exchange of a ring or bangle and their respective horoscopes. The day and venue of marriage will be fixed on this day. Sometimes they conduct the marriage in the bride's house or in the local community hall or in some auditoriums usually somewhere near the girl's residence.

On the day of marriage, the bridegroom and his relatives go to the venue of marriage in specially arranged vehicles. The bride's house and surroundings are neatly decorated and adorned. Usually, a *pandal* is erected in front of the house and the marriage takes place there. A priest, who is locally available to all castes, conducts the *pooja* and sanctifies the *talichain* and garlands. In the case of the Christians, the priest of a church administers the sacrament of matrimony.

Among the Brahmins, the Brahmin priests themselves perform the marriage rites. Among the Christians the Priest's ecclesiastic role is paramount and the religious rituals are followed strictly without considering anyone's financial status. Yet local influence, sanctions and prohibitions of different cultural groups shape the institution of marriage of different castes and communities.

Earlier and now there is no uniformity in the marriage formalities of different castes and communities of the village. However, some common elements have evolved in the present day among all the castes and communities. Patrilocal residence, and the patrilineal system of inheritance and descent are common today.

With the introduction of a fixed age for marriage by the Government, 18 and 21 for the female and male respectively, marriages are conducted only after attaining these ages. Formerly most of the castes and communities conducted the marriage of girls between "10 and 20", whereas for men it was "15 to 20". The marital age of men and women has risen today to 18 to 28 for women and 21 to 31 for men.

Monogamy

At present, the most common form of marriage is monogamy in which an individual has a single wife at any given time. Arranged marriage takes place after inter-familial discussions is the normal practice. Non-arranged marriages also take place without the consent and/or inter-familial discussion. This type of marriage takes place usually in the case of inter-caste or love marriages.

In general, inter-caste marriage and love marriages are very rare. Legal divorce is also very rare but abandoning a spouse without legal intervention has also occurred. Extramarital relations rarely exist in the covert level and nobody would admit it if one formally inquires about it, though it is pointed out that such instances have taken place within the village. The extramarital relationship has often resulted in the separation of the spouses.

Endogamy

The strict observance of the caste system prevails in marriages. During marriages, people give importance to their traditional beliefs. Although there have been crucial changes in the occupational scene and in the solidarity among the villagers manifest reluctance to practice inter-caste marriages. They consider marriages within the caste more feasible than inter-caste marriages. Usually marriages are endogamous.

Inter-dining of different caste groups in marriages is also becoming very common presently. Earlier, inter-dining was a matter of discussion among scholars. But today, referring to it is irrelevant because so much social change has taken place in the village life. At present, almost all communities possess common cultural traits as far as their life-style is concerned. But, at the same time people are becoming much more conscious about the traditional creeds, customs and manners of each caste group and community. The Christian marriages are generally posh in nature. But, most of their marriages take place in churches according to their religious rites.

Inter-Caste Marriages

As far as the inter-caste marriages, the basic factors that lead to inter-caste marriages are love, ideology, sexual urge, conflicts in family, and mental abnormalities. There are instances of inter-caste marriages in the village but most of them are basically love marriages.

The economic condition has helped a number of youngsters to conduct their own as well as their sister's or brother's marriages in a fairly good manner. Nevertheless, inter-caste or inter-religious marriages have not been encouraged so far. Most of the people go on caste or religious lines as far as their marriage, family and other aspects of life are concerned.

Economic Possessiveness

Empirically, the improvement in the economic condition reflects in every aspect of the life of the villagers. However, marriages are becoming expensive. Their economy seems to be stable, and it is reflected in their dress, ornaments, feast, decorations and in other aspects of marriage.

The marriages are conducted in *pandal* erected in front of the house. Almost all communities invite people of other castes and communities to the marriages. Nevertheless, some inter-caste marriages have been identified within the village. But, today there is no caste or religious restrictions for joining the celebrations of marriages of other caste people.

Dowry

Dowry system was prevalent in the olden days too, however, it was not so strong as of today. Four or five decades ago, groom's relatives did not have to ask for dowry, for it was really a gift from the parents to the girl. Families of average income group give five to ten sovereigns worth of gold ornaments, whereas the affluent families give about twenty to twenty five sovereigns worth of gold ornaments. The bride is gifted with brass and steel vessels for domestic use. In the past no girl remained unmarried due to lack of dowry as of the present day.

At present, with the elaborate and expensive pomp and show of marriages, the dowry system has become an unavoidable element of the institution of marriage. In the case of dowry all villagers, except the northern villages, in Kerala are similar. Dowry is paid in cash or as ornaments or both. Since many villagers have moved to the gold jewellery work, the use of gold ornaments such as necklaces, bangles, rings, chains, etc., has become very common now.

Dowry causes heavy expenses for the bride's family, for the groom it is his life's main chance for economic gain. There are differences among castes and communities in asking for or accepting dowry. For example, most of the Christians and a good number of Ezhavas give or accept dowry according to prior discussions and inter-familial decisions taken by both the bride's and groom's families.

In many cases, marriages take place only after deciding the amount of dowry. Apart from this, when many of the families became affluent due to the occupational shift, the amount of dowry paid has steadily increased during the last two decades.

Dowry in the form of gold ornaments of 25 sovereigns or 50 or 100 sovereigns, i.e., 200 grams or 400 or 800 grams is a common measure. (One sovereign is equal to eight grams). A mediocre family gives dowry ranging from 25 to 50 sovereigns gold ornaments. Moreover, some demand or offer cash ranging from 50 thousand to one or more lakhs.

Marriage is predominantly a family concern more than the sole interest of the bride and groom. Dowry helps the daughter and her husband to set up an economically stable household; however, it becomes a crisis for the girl's family in many instances. If the girl is not much educated the groom's family asks for more dowry. On the contrary, if the girl is beautiful the groom's party may not demand dowry, beauty seemingly compensating dowry!

In general, the economic concerns during marriages have increased now. It is due to the impact of the occupational mobility and the improvement in the economic condition of the people due to occupational diversification.

Impact of Occupational Diversification on Family

The family is a basic and universal social institution (Oswalt 1986:136). The family is the most important primary group, and it comes into existence when a man and a woman establish conjugal relationship, which is established through the institution of marriage. A number of scholars have provided definitions for the institution of family. According to Harris (1983:6), family is a social group that conforms to and exhibits a particular society's culture of domestic life. "The family is a social unit consisting minimally of parents and children. Families ... are as nearly universal as marriage. The members of a family (particularly the parents and their young children) usually live in a common household and acknowledge certain reciprocal rights and obligations, especially with regard to economic activity" (Ember and Ember 1985: 174). "The family is...characterized by common residence, economic cooperation, and reproduction. It includes adults of both sexes, at least two of whom maintain a socially approved sexual relationship, and one or more children, their own or adopted, of the sexually cohabiting adults" (Murdock 1949:1). "The family is a group of persons united by the ties of marriage, blood or adoption, constituting a single household, interacting and communicating with each other in their respective roles of husband and wife, mother and father, son and daughter, brother and sister" (Burgess and Locke: 1945) (quoted in Dubey 1955:15).

Family is the basic unit of the society and its economic condition helps the members of the family to find a better way of living. "The family is a social group consisting of married adults who usually live together, cooperate in economic activities, and share the rearing of children, who complete the membership" (Oswalt 1986:136). The family has undergone a number of changes due to the influence of education, occupational diversification, and contact with other societies and the development or welfare programmes implemented by the Government.

Family Size

The family size varies from household to household and it is based on the number of male or female spouses in each house. However, the total number of husband, wife and children, and the combination varies within a single household from time to time. Such changes can be observed in different households of the same caste/community. At present, the number of members of a family varies from one (1) to thirteen (13). The family types include nuclear families, broken nuclear families, and extended families. The most stable form of families is the nuclear type. The broken-nuclear families and extended families are only a transitional category, since the members of these categories mostly prefer nuclear families.

At present, the post-marital residence pattern is patrilocal or virilocal, i.e., the wife lives with the husband in his house. The extended families prevalent among the people are patrilocal extended families, i.e., two or more nuclear families are affiliated through an extension of father-son relationship.

In the first half of the 20th century, the joint families and extended families were the common types of family among most of the castes and communities, particularly among the affluent groups. As far as the poor people were concerned, they lived in small joint families or extended families. Besides, some of them had to depend on the their landlords and agriculturists and other affluent groups in the village for their livelihood. It is a fact that the joint family and extended family systems have merits as well as demerits. In such a family, all the members could not satisfy their personal desires. However, responsibilities were distributed among all the members of the joint family, which was an advantage. During the days of joint families, the house types of the affluent families were the *nalukettu* type. But, these types of houses and the joint family system disappeared with the introduction of Land Reform and the Hindu Succession Act, 1956.

The higher castes such as Warriar, Nayar, Menon, etc., have completely shifted to patrilineal system. But, in the past when there were more number of extended families, they were following the matrilineal system. The lower castes like Ezhava, Kalarikurup, Viswakarma, Marasari, Kallasari, Musari, Thattan, Karuvan, Pandaran, Kudumbi, Perumannan, Pulaya, Vettuvan, Paraya, etc., followed the patrilocal residence and patrilineal system of descent and inheritance and still continue to do so.

Structural Change of Families

At present, the family structure is changing, and there is a greater tendency towards nuclear family. In the recent past, the extended families were the common type. The shift from extended families to nuclear families is the major change today. Nevertheless, the nuclear families

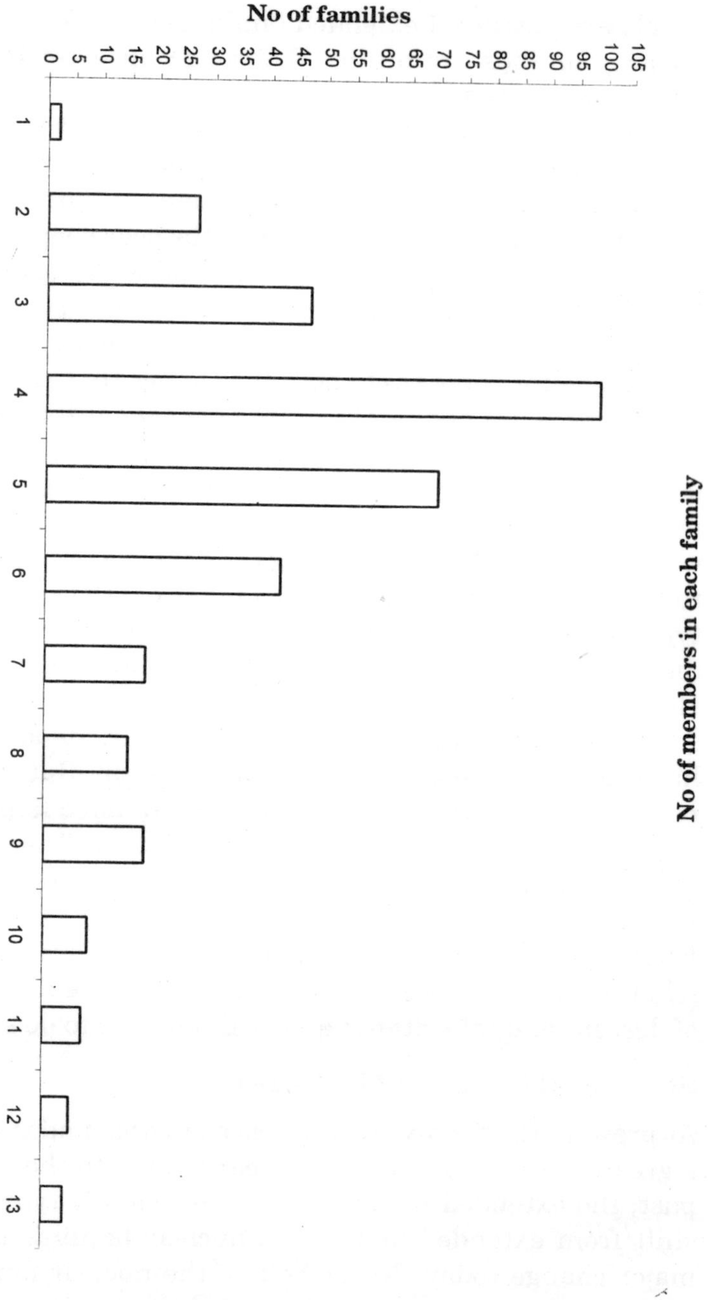

Figure 2
Sizes of Families

are also changing to extended families and also to broken nuclear families. Basically, the people prefer nuclear families, though a considerable number of them cannot establish nuclear families due to financial reasons.

When occupational shift towards goldwork, became a reality most of the youngsters come forward to this job and in many families they took the responsibilities themselves. Thus the familial responsibility virtually shifted to the youngsters of the households.

Figure 3
Distribution of Families by Family Types

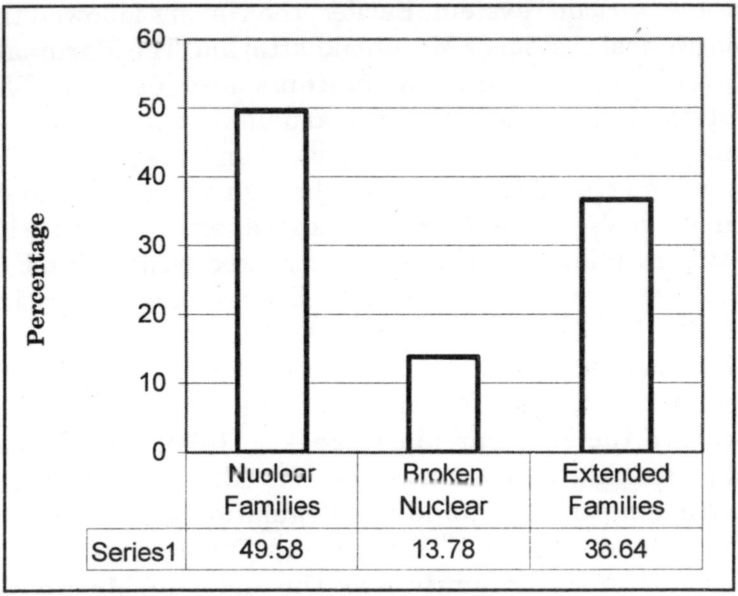

Table 1
Distribution of Households by Family Types

Family Types	*No of Households*	*Percentage*
Nuclear Families	180	49.58
Extended Families	133	36.64
Broken Nuclear Families	50	13.78

There are 363 households and the family types vary from household to household. The nuclear family is a common type of family, and broken nuclear family is the rare type. There are 49.58 per cent Nuclear Families, 13.78 per cent Broken Nuclear Families, and 36.64 per cent Extended Families in the village.

Apart from the change due to occupational diversification, there are other strong measures like the Hindu Succession Act, 1956, which have been the causative factor for the change of family structure. The later is, of course, a factor for the disappearance of the Marumakkattayam (Matrilineal system) and the joint family (*tarwad*) system. Earlier, the Nayars followed the matrilineal system or Marumakkattayam. The Marumakkattayam is a body of customs and usages. The outstanding feature of the Marumakkattayam is that inheritance was through nephews and nieces and the members traced their descent through a common female ancestress. "The Marumakkattayam...essentially customary law and there are no sacred writing binding on the followers of these systems. Even prior to the passing of the Hindu Succession Act, the common law of Marumakkattayam...has been considerably modified by the statutory law. The main enactments modifying the law are the Malabar Marriage Act, 1896; the Madras Marumakkattayam Act, 1932; the Mapilla Marumakkattayam Act, 1939; and the Regulation of the State of Travancore-Cochin. "(Diwan and Diwan 1995: 406). *Tarwad* or joint family was the units of Marumakkattayam, which was based on matriarchal system. "Mayne [in his book Hindu Law and Usage: 972-73] writes thus about the tarwad. *Tarwad* is the name given to the joint family consisting of males and females, all descended in the female line from a common ancestress. It is an undivided family governed by the Marumakkattayam law, the customary law of Malabar. Its outstanding feature is that for the purpose of inheritance descent is traced through the female line. A *tarwad* may consist of two or more branches known as *tavazhies* each *tavazhi* or branch consisting of one of the female members of the *tarwad* and her descendants in the female line." (quoted in Diwan & Diwan) The law of succession of Marumakkattayam had been changed by legislative enactments.

Genealogical Structure

The changes in the types of families can be depicted genealogically. With the help of the genealogical analysis a comparative picture of the earliest or rare types of family and the current and most popular family typology is being attempted in the following pages. The structural change of families and its gradual transformation can be depicted genealogically.

Extended families have a complex structure and the Nuclear families have a simple structure. Complex structure restricts individual freedom in decision-making regarding family matters. Often, the family head takes decisions in an extended family; however, the opinion of others is sought on many occasions. Whereas in simple structures, the number of family members is limited from 3 to 7, and the individual interests of the family members is satisfied considerably when it is compared with the extended family or complex structure of the family.

"A family that consists of two or more nuclear... families joined by blood ties over two or more generations is called an extended family. This form was the most common family type in traditional societies and that combines families of orientation and procreation into an integrated composite. An extended family is able to maintain more stability than the other forms as new members are added and others die or move elsewhere" (Oswalt 1986:138-139). "An extended family consists of two or more nuclear families affiliated through an extension of the parent-child relationship rather than of the husband-wife relationship, i.e., by joining the nuclear family of a married adult to that of his parents" (Murdock 1949:2). The extended family consists of two or more single-parent, monogamous, polygynous, or polyandrous families linked by a blood bond. The extended family consists most commonly of a married couple and one or more of the married children, all living under the same roof and consuming food cooked in the same kitchen. The constituent nuclear families are linked through the parent-child tie. However, an extended family is sometimes composed of families linked through a sibling tie. Such a family might consist of two married brothers, their wives, and their children. Extended families may be quite large, consisting many nuclear families and including three generations (Ember and Ember 1985: 175).

Extended Family

Extended families provide a complex genealogical structure, whereas nuclear families provide a simple structure. As far as the village is concerned, the number of extended families is comparatively small. The occupational diversification and the occupational mobility, the family welfare programmes and a number of rural housing programmes, and the Hindu succession Act of 1956 were some of the reasons for the change in the family structure.

The following are the genealogical representations of extended families in the village. At present, 36.64 per cent of the families belong to this category.

[*Note*: In all the Genealogical diagrams included here, the grey coloured are residing in a single household. The white coloured are not included in the present family structure. Of these (white) some are deceased and some stay in separate household].

Figure 4
Genealogy of 11-member family

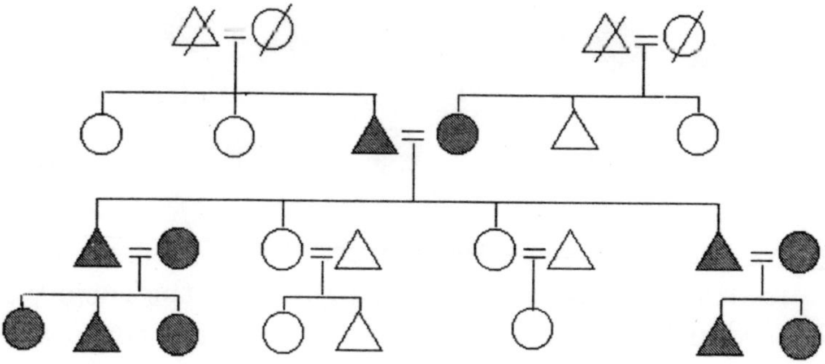

Figure 5
Genealogy of 12-member family

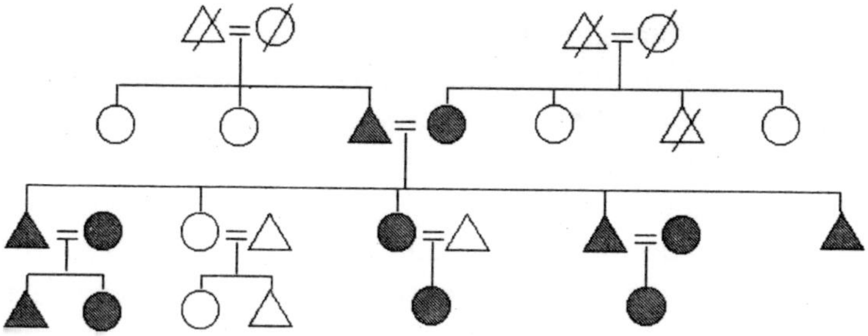

Nuclear Families

The four member Nuclear families and five member Nuclear families are the typical family types of the present day. Nevertheless, the stability of nuclear families is a problem as the chances are higher for breaking the nuclear families due to death of either of the spouses or with the marriage of the son(s) or daughter(s).

"The nuclear family serves as the centre of a child's social universe - in it he or she is reared, is cared for,

Figure 6
Genealogy of 4 and 5 member family

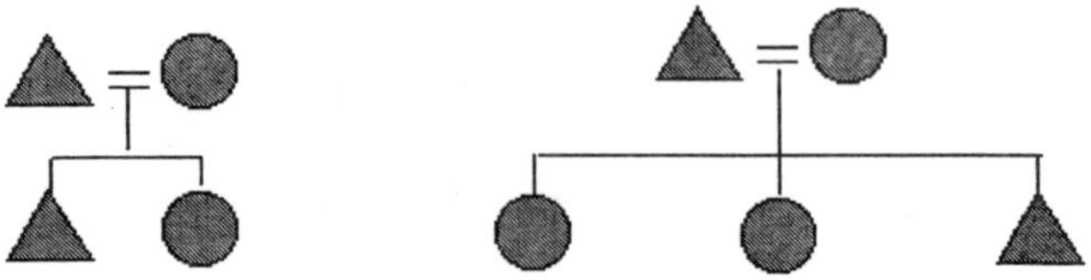

grows up, and learns the culture. Sexual relations and hence reproduction and the continuity of the society are focused in the family. It serves as an economic corporation, owning property and producing (or acquiring) and consuming food" (Keesing 1981:267). According to Murdock (1949:1) "nuclear family, consists typically of a married man and woman with their offspring, although in individual cases one or more additional persons may reside with them".

The excessive growth of nuclear families in the village is due to the economic uplift of the people. The occupational diversification and occupational shift are the major reasons for the improvement of the economy. The growth of goldwork helped them to work day and night, according to demand, and this work culture is also a prime reason. In ordinary circumstances, there are limitations to work according to the nature of occupations. When the limitations are removed, the people accumulate wealth as well as own independent houses.

In general, the economic possessiveness alone is the major factor that helped them to build independent houses for the minimum family units. Nevertheless, the nuclear families are fragile due to a number of reasons and easily form broken nuclear families.

Broken Nuclear Families

According to the Figure 7, the only daughter is married and widow the stays with her son. It is a broken nuclear

Figure 7
Genealogy of 2-member family

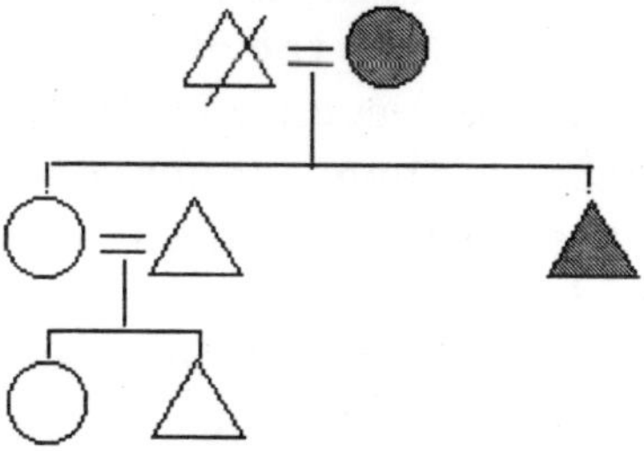

Figure 8
Genealogy of 2-member family

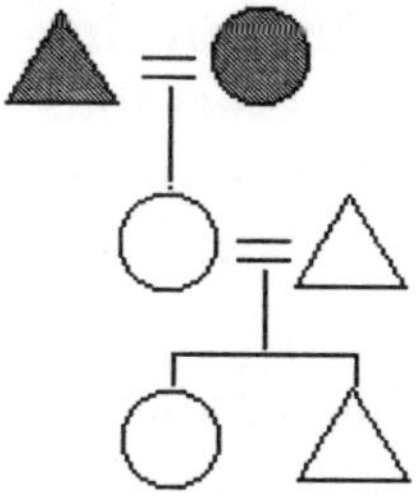

Fig ure 9
Genealogy of 2-member family

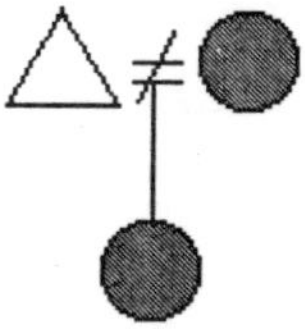

family. In the example given in Figure 8, the only daughter has got married and is staying with her husband according to the patrilocal law. This resulted in the broken nuclear family.

The Figure 9 is also an example of a broken nuclear family in this village. In this particular instance, his husband divorced the woman, and the woman and her daughter (minor) live together.

Transitional Types of Families

At present, the nuclear families are the most common type of families, and this shows the attitude and aspiration of the people. Though the people wish to perpetuate nuclear families, a number of them cannot continue it for a long time. It may be because of the death of a spouse or due to the marriage of daughter(s). Accidents also break nuclear families. Thus, it can be seen that there are a number of transitional categories of families without any structural stability, and categorization rather unnecessary.

The family structure changes with marriage and financial condition helps the people to conduct the marriage of their children in time. It is a cyclic process and "each type of family is established through marriage, and the person who is the product of one becomes the producer in the other" (Oswalt 1986:136).

Figure 10
Genealogy of 5-member family

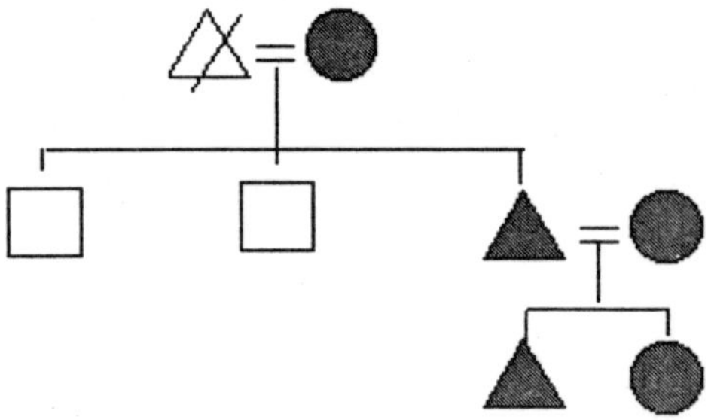

Impact of Occupational Diversification on Education

The impact of occupational diversification on education is a critical aspect, as it has been one among the factors of change in the village. With the growth of secular or non-traditional occupations, educational attainment has become indispensable. The families perform educational functions such as schooling the children for formal education. Enculturation, primarily of young ones, normally takes place within the family. The non-formal and informal education also takes place within or from the family, to a great extent.

The villages are not an isolated whole. Each and every nook and corner of our country is under the pressure and influence of development programmes. A major change observed in the village is the shift of traditional technology to modern technology in every sphere of life and culture. Science and technology and modern education have enabled the people to find new occupations. Finally, education in turn has supported the enhancement of occupational diversification.

At present, the educational status of the people of the village has been considerably improved. Here, the term education is used to refer to the formal education and status is evaluated in terms of the courses completed by the people. "Formal education prepares individuals for a particular style of life characteristic of a status group. It acts as a differentiating agency as it seeks to maintain and supply appropriately socialised individuals to each one of the strata" (Rao 1972:131).

Almost all people have participated in the State literacy programmes, yet some do not know how to read and write. There are a number of unschooled people belonging to the age group of 30-34 and above (Refer Table 2). However, there are only 6.25 per cent people belonging to the unschooled and literate category. People belonging to the age group of 30-34 and above show a low educational status in the village. All the people of the age group of 25-29 are educated. The gap in terms of higher education in the village is very high. Dropout in the Pre Degree and Degree levels is also very frequent. Technical education such as ITI, ITC, and Polytechnic Diplomas among the people is also improving.

Table 2
Educational Status of the People

Educational Status	*Un Schooled & Literate*		*Lower Primary School*		*Upper Primary School*		*High School*		*Pre-Degree & Plus two*		*Degree*		*Post Graduation*		*Professional Courses*		*Technical Education*		*Total Per cent*
Age Group	M	F	M	F	M	F	M	F	M	F	M	F	M	F	M	F	M	F	
0.4			15	12															
5.9			62	57	5	3													
10.14			5	3	48	46	30	30		1									
15.19			1	1	8	3	31	31	13	29	2	8			1		4	1	
20.24			4	1	23	6	55	46	14	18	13	9	1	1	3	2	7	1	
25.29			5	8	19	17	57	62	11	9	12	9	4	3	3	1	7	2	
30.34	1	1	6	12	28	24	49	45	6	5	6	3	1		1	2	2		
35.39	1	2	12	14	22	18	32	30	3	1	3	3			1	1	1		
40.44	2	4	11	11	15	8	28	16	2		1					1	3		
45.49	1	5	11	9	8	14	14	14	1				1	1	2		1	1	
50.54	4	12	8	19	10	10	6	6	1		1				1				
55.59	5	9	22	11	6	7	9	4			1		1				1		
60.64	4	8	12	19	4	5	5	3					2				1		
65.69	2	13	18	20	4	3	3								2		1	1	
70.74	5	7	6	9	4		1												
75.79	2	14	5	4		1													
80.85	2	5	6		1	1													
Total	29	80	209	210	205	166	320	287	51	63	39	32	10	5	14	7	28	6	1761
Percentage	1.65	4.6	11.86	11.91	11.63	9.42	18.2	16.3	2.89	3.57	2.2	1.8	0.6	0.28	0.8	0.4	1.58	0.35	100

The technical and higher educational attainments of the older generation (40-44 to 65-69) is lower than that of the present generation. It is striking to note that all the children up to 14 years have received and/or are receiving elementary education.

According to the household survey, 23.77 per cent of the people attained Lower Primary education and 21.05 per cent achieved Upper Primary education. 34.44 per cent people had High School education. 6.46 per cent of the people had Pre Degree and 4.02 per cent had Degree level education. Only 0.88 per cent people are educated upto the Post Graduate level. As far as the Professional Courses are concerned, only 1.2 per cent of the villagers had achieved professional education, whereas 1.93 per cent people have attained Technical education.

Although the educational level of the people is very low, many of them lead a better life, and it is obviously by means of the diversified occupations. The occupational mobility is very high. Many youngsters without any caste prejudice have taken up the traditional art of manufacturing ornaments. About 15 years ago this was done purely by the goldsmiths in the village. But today, many higher caste and lower caste Hindus have entered into this profession.

The educational institutions and other allied organisations have become the avenues of occupational diversification in Kerala. Varghese (1999) has provided some significant points regarding the occupational diversification in the field of education along with the development of the education and educational institutions. According to him, "Many community-based organisations of Christians, Nairs [Nayars] and Ezhavas started establishing their own schools and colleges. However, admissions to these educational institutions were open to members of all communities. One important policy statements of the government in 1887 prescribing minimum qualifications for jobs had a positive impact on the demand for education. Qualification-based job selection process cut the caste barriers. Since education was not equitably distributed among communities, such a policy meant competitions among various communities to establish schools and confer jobs, which were based on educational qualifications. This has contributed to increased community involvement in establishing educational institutions in Kerala" (Varghese 1999: 372-373).

With occupational diversification, education has become an essential criterion for achieving new or secular occupations. In a later phase, though a number of people got educated, unemployment was the result. Then the people started giving more importance to income generating occupations whether it was traditional or secular occupations. Many of the villagers succeeded in this regard. This helped the people to achieve better financial position and its reflections have reached in almost all spheres of their life style. Further, they are providing better education to their children. These are the major inferences from the village regarding occupational diversification and its impact on education.

In the foregoing pages an attempt has been made to draw an outline of the changes in the village. The occupational shift from caste-bound to caste-free occupations was mainly due to economic pressure. Most of the traditional occupations were not income generating and therefore those occupations were discouraged. Under these circumstances, depending upon the profit from the occupations, a villager moves out of his caste-bound occupations.

Inter-relations of castes or communities within a culture area are fervent, but outside the culture area inter-relations are not so strong. The whole of Kerala can be taken as a cultural area for its particular language and solidarity. The particular cultural behaviour of this cultural area, Kerala, is distinct from other areas in the country. The frequency of interactions among the people of this area, on the basis of caste and community, is very limited whereas the frequency of inter-relations and interactions in terms of economy or commercial activities is more in the present day. Migratory character of the people, especially goldworkers, to different cities paved the way for acculturation and culture change. This resulted in socio-cultural change.

The people of a linguistic zone whether it is a village, or a taluk, interact with outsiders mainly for monetary reasons. Caste and kinship motivations work only within a limited cultural milieu. The present study analyses micro-elements and attempts to draw macro-generalisations.

Any change in the constituent elements of culture reflects on the composite culture, which gets stipulated and become overt or covert in socio-cultural change. The constituent elements of culture are usually referred to as cultural traits. The simple and the smallest unit of culture is the cultural trait. These cultural traits develop concurrently and collect together like a cluster and gain their importance in terms of the degree of significance that they leave for the behaviour of human beings. This bunch of traits is referred to as culture complex. Therefore, the change of culture traits or change in the composition of the culture traits can be referred to as culture change. When culture traits change, socio-cultural change becomes a reality and it can be observed in the way of life of the people. The pattern of change could be identified according to the present study and it is based on a village in Central Kerala and on the occupational diversification and socio-cultural change.

'Occupational diversification' can be defined as the development or proliferation or multiplication or

Figure 11
Educational Status

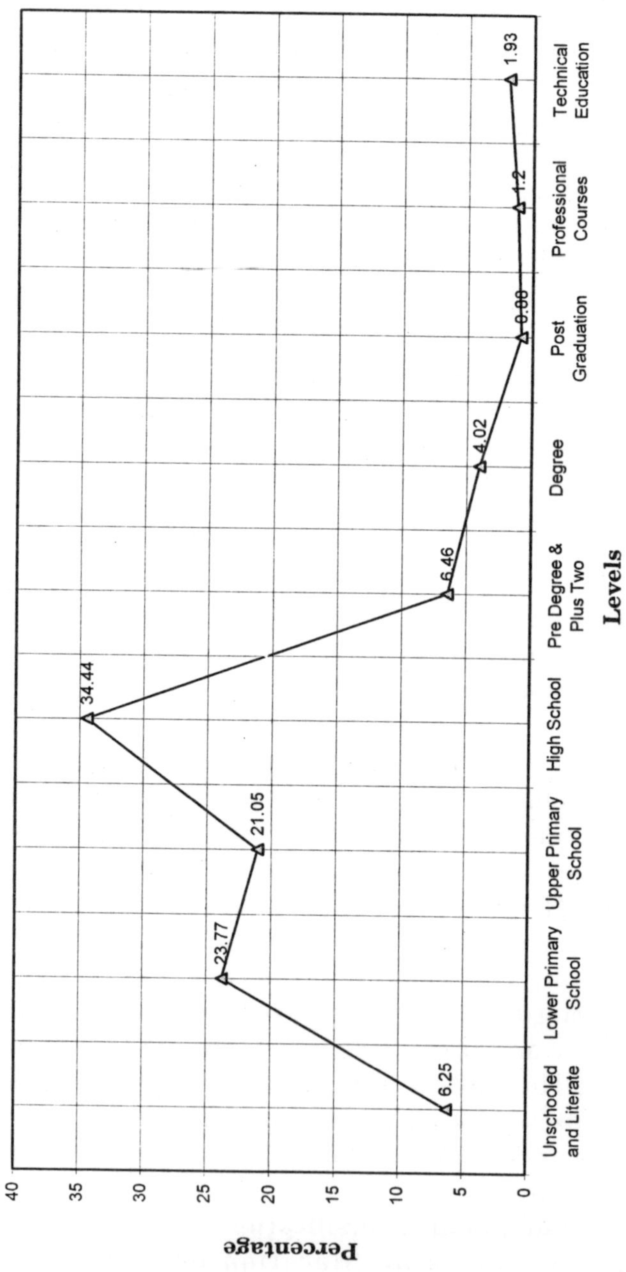

diversification of occupations due to the introduction or adoption of new occupations into the existing pool of occupations for new social requirements. Occupations are modified according to human needs, when the existing social systems or network of social relations or social institutions fail to meet the existing requirements, or when new material wants are felt for a better living. Means of livelihood or occupation itself is a part of culture. At present, the new occupational opportunities have been the basis of the present change. The functional role of castes and communities is being transformed to accept new changes in the socio-cultural realm.

There are two major directions of occupational change, occupational mobility outside the caste system and within the caste system. The first development is mainly due to modern education, science and technology and the occupational opportunities emerging. The second, occupational mobility within the caste system is an alternative developed due to the inadequate development of the modern system in the rural areas.

Among the traditional caste occupations, upward mobility and downward mobility have been identified in the village. The upward mobility of occupations is a general aspect that is available in many villages of the Malayalam linguistic zone, whereas the downward mobility is rather a rare phenomenon. This instance is quite contrary to the concept of 'Dominant Caste' and also the concept 'Sanskritization'.

For example, a few lower castes have adopted the traditional occupation of a Backward Caste, namely, the Thattan and at the same time, a few upper castes also adopted the traditional occupation of the Thattan. This feature is contrary to the concept of caste system, the concept of Dominant caste, and the concept of Sanskritization. The rules of caste permit a caste group to perpetuate its own traditional occupation and services and or duties. The concepts used by Srinivas were useful in explaining the patterns of change of Indian village communities. He pointed out that changes are taking place among the lower caste groups due to their imitation and/ or adoption of the way of life of the dominant castes or higher castes in the *Varna* model.

Earlier, the villagers were confined to their own villages to satisfy most of their needs and only a few like traders, etc., were exposed to urban centres. But, now almost all people are exposed to urban centres or cities through various means. Apart from traders, those who work in Govt. offices, private business establishments, hospitals, colleges, schools, and the students are regularly going to the towns, urban centres, and cities and are in regular contact with others. This is due to the cultural contact with the towns and urban centres today, and only a small per cent of the villagers keep away from the accumulation of different cultural traits of a heterogeneous population from the surrounding villages and urban centres.

The major elements, which helped in bringing about cultural change, are namely, education, politics, communication networks, developmental programmes, and cultural contact through travel. All these aspects necessitate opportunities for continuous cultural contacts with different cultural composites and this in turn changes the life in villages, towns or urban centres.

A recent study on a village, Kottakkal, in Malappuram District in Kerala, conducted by Bhanu and Mahendrakumar (2000) also delineates occupational diversification and occupational mobility. The growth of non-traditional occupation within the Kottakkal village is mainly with the beginning of the Kottakkal Arya Vaidya Sala, an Ayurveda medicine manufacturing industry and hospital. The impact of emigration and out-migration of the people are discussed in that study, which shows a compatible nature of change as far as the present study is concerned.

As anthropology is an eclectic subject, the findings of Sivaram are very important. Sivaram (1990) conducted a sociological study on the occupational mobility among the Backward Classes of Cuddopah District of Rayalaseema region, an urban area, in Andhra Pradesh. He argued, "Any moving away may be termed as mobility, whether it be the change of residence, or of an occupation or of a social stratum". Education is also a factor for occupational mobility and extent of literacy and educational attainment has continued to rise from one generation to another. The study also indicates that the caste system as a determinant in occupational choice is still a dynamic force; and that there are castes, which are occupationally oriented in the sense that the selected [for the study] Backward Castes are following their occupations.

The present study shows a compatible trend of occupational mobility pointed out by Sivaram but it has been identified among all caste groups in the village. Further, the occupational choice in the village is also made by economic considerations as pointed out by Freeman (1977), Sivaram (1990), and others.

Economic aspect of the traditional occupations is also important because people continue their occupations in order to meet their livelihood. In general, people have abandoned their traditional occupation for two major reasons: one, due to meagre financial gain; two, due to inferior social status. This type of occupational shift has been identified in the contiguous villages and other parts of the Thrissur district in Kerala. The economic aspect has greater significance as the people are engaged in all services and jobs for a livelihood. Once the economic side of the occupations declines, people move onto other areas of occupations for higher wages and thereby lead a better life.

Sinha's (1992) paper entitled 'Occupational Mobility in West Bengal with Special Reference to Moyra Caste' also gives a particular type of occupational mobility, and it explains that in ancient period the profession of sweetmeat production was exclusively meant for the Moyra caste and they provided food to the orthodox Hindus. The Brahmins used to take drinking water from them. When traditional occupations of the Moyras became unprofitable, as they were preparing the sweetmeat in the traditional way, they adopted different professions. Meanwhile, a few members of other castes have adopted machines and modern technology for the production of sweetmeat. The economic backwardness of the Moyras compelled them to work in such sweetmeat shops apart from other vocations. At present, about 75 per cent of the other castes are engaged in this profession. Sinha has not provided any theoretical explanation for this pattern of change. The occupational shift identified in the present research is similar to the above pattern. However, the hierarchical position of the Moyra and the Thattan, the traditional goldsmith, is different.

Occupational diversification has been a significant factor for the present change. This diversification provides new job opportunities other than their traditional occupations to the villagers. Occupational diversification is an outcome of various socio-cultural innovations. According to Barnett (1953:7) (quoted in Oswalt 1986:190) two kinds of change, innovative and noninnovative, occur in every culture. An innovation is any thought, behavior, or thing that is qualitatively different from forms existing previously. "Noninnovative change is a minor alteration of an existing trait. The trait may change in size or style, but its basic qualities remain intact...Noninnovative change occurs in mental and behavioural areas as well. This can be seen readily in language usage"(Oswalt 1986:190).

It is quite significant that the term goldsmithy has also been changed after the non-traditional caste and communities shifted to the traditional occupation of the goldsmiths. Non-traditional goldworkers prefer to use the term goldwork. They do not use the term goldsmithy. Non-goldsmiths use the term goldwork instead of goldsmithy. *Thattapani* (goldsmithy) became *swarnappani* (goldwork).

Sanskritization and Change

When there is Sanskritization, mobility occurs within the framework of caste, whereas Westernisation implies mobility outside the framework of caste. Srinivas used the term, 'Sanskritization' to describe the process of cultural mobility in the traditional social structure. In his study he found that lower castes, in order to raise their position in the caste hierarchy, adopted some customs of the Brahmins and gave up some of their own, which were considered to be impure by the higher castes. He redefined that "Sanskritization is the process by which a "low" Hindu caste, or tribal or other group, changes its customs, ritual, ideology and way of life in the direction of a high, and frequently of a "twice born" caste. Generally such changes are followed by a claim to a higher position in the caste hierarchy than that traditionally conceded to the claimant caste by the local community" (Srinivas, 1995).

Ishwaran's (1968) empirical study on the Shivpur village examines the applicability of Srinivas's concepts, Sanskritization and Westernisation. Ishwaran logically criticises those concepts and points out that, "Srinivas considers 'Sanskritization' as the process whereby mobility takes place within the framework of caste. He maintains that dominant castes accelerate or retard these processes; by a dominant caste, he means one that is numerically superior, ritually superior, and controls the economy of the village. It is our [Ishwaran, et al.] thesis that the hypothesised relationship between supposed caste dominants and some process like sanskritization is simply inapplicable to Shivpur. One caste, ...the Lingayat, has a majority, is ritually superior to the others, and is relative control of farming, the basis of the village economy. But it cannot say to be ascendancy over the other castes. Thus it is not in a position to speed up or retard some mythical 'sanskritization' process. Shivpur is becoming neither 'sanskritized' nor 'westernised', but is adapting its traditional order to meet the exigencies of modern living without abandoning or changing its traditional character in any essential respect" (Ishwaran, 1968:30-31).

The present study identified that the caste is still functioning in many aspects of life and culture. Though some of the traditional occupations have declined, all the traditional occupations cannot perish due to the inadequate growth of the secular occupations. Moreover, a number of traditional occupations have ample demand even today.

Occupational rigidity is non-existent today. Moreover, at present there are no restrictions in selecting and eliminating any occupation, as a result of which many caste groups have adopted different caste occupations. Ezhavas have adopted carpentry, masonry, goldwork, etc. Nayars, Asari, Karuvan, Perumannan, Musari, etc., have adopted goldwork.

There is a shift of emphasis from the concept of the dignity of occupation to the economic advantage. This was found to be the one and the only reason for the occupational mobility towards goldwork in and around the village. Upward mobility and downward mobility, within the caste occupations, are taking place in a big way. This is a rare instance where the applicability of the concept Sanskritization becomes impossible.

Sharma (1994:204) says, "Sanskritization is applicable to the understanding of group mobility vis-à-vis caste structure particularly with reference to socio-cultural behaviour patterns. Sanskritization is to be used as a tool of analysis regarding dominant castes or groups and caste ranking and ranks of the sanskritizing castes. Sanskritization does not necessarily reduce 'economic inequalities' nor does it challenge caste hierarchy, however, it symbolizes an increased sense of awareness among the non-privileged sections". The model of Sanskritization for lower castes is not always the Brahmin. Instead in most of the areas the dominant caste serves as the model for Sanskritization (Hasnain 1991:227).

To the best of my knowledge, Sanskritization has taken place in the village in the third quarter of the 20th century. Some of the lower castes below the rank of the Nayars (example: Ezhuthachan, Kammalar, etc.) have imitated the rituals of the Nayars and the Ambalavasi group of castes. From this instance, it is possible to assert that the lower castes have at least adopted some of the behaviours of the higher castes. But it has not provided them a higher status in the local caste hierarchy. It is a mere ambition of the lower castes to behave like a higher caste, and the very behaviour has provided them a better acceptance only when they go out of the village where appearance is essentially useful to have good approach from others.

At present, Sanskritization is not taking place in the village. The present day pattern of change is a very complicated one. However, in the earlier period, Social reforms were the fundamental reason for a number of changes in the village and the whole of Kerala; and the village, virtually, is a microcosm of Kerala.

Among the Ezhavas, the changes have happened because of the social reforms launched by the SNDP in the first quarter of the last century. Sri Narayana Guru (1856-1928) founded the *Sri Narayana Dharma*

Paripalana Yogam (SNDP), in 1903, and he persuaded the Ezhavas to give up the observance of such irrational practices as *talikettu kalyanam* (pseudo marriage), *tirandukuli* (puberty ceremony), *pulikudi* (taking sour drinks during pregnancy), etc., which stood in the way of their progress. A similar kind of reform movement took place among the Pulayas too. Ayyankali (1866-1941), a Pulaya leader, drew inspiration from the work of Sri Narayana Guru, founded the *Sadhu Jana Paripalana Yogam* (in 1907) with the aim of working for the social uplift of the Scheduled Castes. The above reform movements made significant impact among the lower castes in the villages in Kerala. Such changes cannot be conceived as Sanskritization as claimed by Srinivas. Srinivas' concept Sanskritization did not mention the changes in caste behaviour due to social reform movements.

Caste Fusion, Sanskritization, and Social Reforms

In most of the villages in Kerala, including the village studied, caste fusion has occurred among a few castes. But the fusion took place only within a major caste and its subcastes. It did not occur at the inter-caste levels. Caste fission has not occurred and/or identified in the village. The caste fusion is the reverse of caste fission or multiplication. The occupation, migration, conflicts within the caste, etc. were some of the major factors for the caste segregations and the formation of sub-castes.

In Kerala, Caste fusion originally occurred as a part of social reform movements in the early phase of the 20th Century. Nevertheless, it has helped the process of occupational diversification considerably. Chattampi Swamikal (1853-1924) could arouse the social consciousness of his own caste, namely, the Nayars. The "Nair Service Society (NSS) was founded in 1914, and its leader Mannath Padmanabhan made many efforts in the moral regeneration of the Nair community by eradicating such social evils as untouchability, subcaste barriers and observance of "irrational social practices" like *talikettukalyanam*, *thirandukuli*, etc." (Menon 1979:202). This helped some of the subcastes among the Nayars to come closer and resulted in the caste fusion.

In olden times, the Vellaima Sudra Nayars among the Nayars of the village were the only caste permitted to come in contact with the Nambutiris. However they were not permitted to dine along with the Nambutiris in a feast. If anybody did so he would be beaten up by his own men. The Vellaima Sudra Nayars did not visit the house of Sudra Nayars, Vattekadan Nayars, and the Pallichan Nayars.

At present, in this village, there are no differences among the four subcastes, namely, the Vellaima Sudra Nayar, Sudra Nayar, Vattekadan Nayar, and the Pallichan Nayar. As the Veluthedath Nayar and the Velakkithala Nayar continue their traditional occupations, namely, washing clothes and haircutting, the higher caste Nayars did not accept them wholeheartedly, as a result of which inter-marriages between the Nayars, and the "Washermen Nayars" and the "Barber Nayars" take place quite rarely. The Vellaima Sudra Nayar, Sudra Nayar, Vattekadan Nayar, and the Pallichan Nayar are known simply as Nayars and many of them are reluctant to reveal the names of their subcaste. Moreover, it has become irrelevant in the changed situation.

The Nayars, Ezhavas and Christians are the major castes and communities in terms of their numerical strength. But, with the advent of social reforms some subcastes among the Nayars fused together and are commonly referred to as Nayars. Therefore, the present number of castes and communities of this village has declined to 32 instead of 35. This has happened due to the caste fusion, which is very unique.

Land Reforms and Sanskritization

In the Kerala situation, Land Reforms also helped to elevate the status of lower castes and the concept of Sanskritization is not relevant to explain the changes that happened among the agrarian and lower castes. In such circumstances the people were not following the culture of either the dominant caste or the higher castes. The Kerala Agrarian Relations Act (1960), the Kerala Land Reforms Act (1963), and the Kerala Land Reforms Act (1969) were the fundamental factors, which put an end to the Janmi system. According to Menon (1979:80), the pace of land reforms quickened after Independence. The abolition of intermediaries and redistribution of land was the aim of land reforms. Tenancy reforms involving security of tenure, fixation of fair rent and conferring of ownership rights on the erstwhile tenants; legislative measures imposing ceiling on holdings and providing for redistribution of land in excess of ceiling; and also given ownership right to *kudikidappukar* or hutment dwellers. All these measures helped a great number of people in villages throughout Kerala.

The Theory of Pecuniarisation

A scientific explanation for occupational diversification has been provided in this book and it is indeed a complex phenomenon. 'Occupational diversification' is defined as the development and/or proliferation and/or multiplication and/or diversification of occupations due to the introduction and/or adoption of new occupations into the existing occupations for novel social requirements. Occupational diversification may emerge and/or is influenced by the reasons such as to compensate for cyclical or seasonal fluctuations in demand and supply and/or desire to maximise profits. In addition, occupations are modified according to human needs, when the existing social systems or network of social relations or social institutions fail to meet the existing requirements, or when new material wants are felt for a better living.

The inference of the present study points out the shift in the concept from the dignity of occupation to the economic advantage. This was the one and the only reason for the occupational mobility towards goldwork, carpentry, etc., in villages. But, that mobility is within the caste occupations, and both downward and upward occupational mobility is taking place greatly. This is a rare instance where the applicability of the concept of Sanskritization becomes impossible. Moreover, Sanskritization does not mention occupational change and its pattern.

At present, economic well-being or wealth of an individual is the main basis for power and prestige in the village more than the prestige attached occupations. *This shift from the old concept of occupations to a new concept provides a pattern and it can be referred to as Pecuniarisation.* Downward and upward occupational mobility pertaining to any particular occupations is the basic character of this phenomenon and this process is taking place all over Kerala. The theory of *Pecuniarisation* includes the same motivation of the two-way process of occupational mobility; where the adoption of the traditional occupation of a caste by any other caste either as an individual or as a group merely with an economic motive is defined as *Pecuniarisation*. Moreover, among a heterogeneous population, the non-caste people also followed some traditional economic activities and they started to adopt other vocations in the line of other people, hence they too possess the very pattern. Therefore, the theory of pecuniarisation is applicable to them also.

"The Indian village is not an isolated entity although it can be regarded as one for empirical investigation" (Verma 1977:15). Therefore, it is hoped that the theoretical explanations provided in this study would be useful for further research and analysis. This microcosmic study reveals that the shift from traditional occupation to new occupations is an underscorable change, and the occupational diversification and occupational mobility are making significant socio-cultural changes in the village life. While new cultural traits are being added to the traditional life style, many traits are being removed from the traditional life style.

There were only a few categories of occupations existed in the village earlier. But with occupational diversification, better occupations are available to the people for their livelihood. This helps them to ameliorate their living conditions to a great extent. Therefore, occupational diversification is a positive factor for the development of society. The finding of this study is that the occupational diversification has utmost importance and plays a vital role in the present socio-cultural change. It has provided better means of livelihood, more earnings, and higher social status. Thus Pecuniarisation has become the order of the day. It is the pattern of social change taking place not only in Kerala but all over India.

6

CONCLUSIONS

The traditional occupations, occupational diversification, pattern of interaction of castes and communities, the change in interaction due to occupational diversification, the impact of occupational diversification, and the socio-cultural change are the pivotal theme of the present study.

For the study and analyses, each caste group has been regarded as an analytical unit. Ishwaran (1968) opined that caste is still functional in determining an individual's occupation in most cases. But, the present study reveals that it is not a determining factor. However, changes in occupation have not become completely free and universal (Bose 1975). Occupational mobility is pervasive and there are no restrictions as it was prevalent in the 19th Century and in the early decades of 20th Century. The economic system of rural India is founded predominantly on the caste's functional specialisation, interdependence and occupational mobility (Dube 1965). Caste in Indian villages to a large extent denotes occupation. Thus, occupational composition of a village is largely determined by caste composition (Madan and Dasgupta 1968). Caste is an endogamous unit and the smallest endogamous units are the subcastes (Mayer 1960). Studies on caste/ traditional occupations pointed out the changes of occupational patterns (Hiramani 1977). The economic change alters the socio-cultural organisation (Epstein 1962). But the aspects namely, social, cultural, religious and economic, inhibit mobility in the village communities (Ansari 1980). At present, the nature of new occupations available to the village people is crucial. The conditions that necessitated such occupations or created as part of the development, and the pattern emerging in acquiring such occupations are also important.

As a prerequisite to the study, an attempt has been made to identify the traditional and/or caste based occupations of the castes and communities, and the changes of their occupations from caste to non-caste and traditional to non-traditional occupations. The occupations of different groups in the village were predominantly based on caste system. In the traditional set up, the members of each caste group had to perform specific functions, and that service and/or occupation was considered traditional occupation.

A comprehensive explanation for occupational diversification has been provided in the chapter on occupational diversification and its complex occurrence. 'Occupational diversification' is defined as the development and/or proliferation and/or multiplication and/or diversification of occupations due to the introduction and/or adoption of new occupations into the existing occupations for novel social requirements. Occupational diversification may emerge and/or is influenced by reasons such as to compensate for cyclical or seasonal fluctuations in demand and supply, and/or desire to maximise profits. In addition, occupations are modified according to human needs, when the existing social systems or network of social relations or social institutions fail to meet the existing requirements, or when new material wants are felt for a better living. Occupation has also become determinant for the differentiation of separate human groups. The traditional occupations and services of the people of this village, like any other Indian village, are mostly caste-based. Therefore, the changes in the caste-based occupations are an important turning point in the social structure of the village. The pattern of livelihood is essentially a major cultural determinant of the people, and it is guided by the occupations.

Occupational diversification has made its impact on family. When occupational shift towards goldwork became a reality, most of the youngsters came forward to do this job and in many families they took up responsibilities themselves. Thus the familial responsibility virtually shifted to the youngsters of the households. The nuclear family is a common type of family and the excessive growth of nuclear families in the village is due to the economic efficiency of the people. The occupational diversification and occupational shift are the major reasons for the improvement of the economy. It also helped the people to build independent houses for the minimum family units.

Impact of occupational diversification on marriage is another important aspect. Inter-caste or inter-religious marriages were not encouraged so far and most of the people go on caste or religious lines as far as their marriage, family and other aspects of life are concerned. The economic efficiency due to occupational diversification has helped a number of youngsters to conduct their own as well as their sister's or brother's marriage in fairly good manner. It also reflects on every aspect of the life of the villagers. Marriages are becoming expensive. Their economy seems to be stable and it is reflected in their dress, ornaments, feast, decorations and in almost all aspects of marriage. Dowry has become an unavoidable element in marriage. Dowry is paid in cash or as ornaments or both. In the case of dowry all the villages, except the northern villages, in Kerala are similar. Since many of the families have become affluent due to the occupational shift, the amount of dowry paid has steadily increased during the last two decades. In general, the economic concerns during marriages have increased now.

The impact of occupational diversification on education is a critical aspect, as it has been one among the factors of change in the village. A major change observed in the village is the shift of traditional technology to modern technology in every sphere of life and culture. Science and technology and modern education have enabled the people to find new occupations. Education has enabled the people to find new occupations. Education has also helped in the enhancement of occupational diversification. With the growth of secular or non-traditional occupations, educational attainment has become an indispensable factor for achieving new or secular occupations. In a later phase, though a number of people got educated, unemployment has been the result. Then the people started giving more importance to income generating occupations whether it is traditional or secular occupations. Many of the villagers succeeded in this regard. This helped them to achieve better financial position and its reflection is discernible in almost all spheres of their life. Further, they are providing better education to their children. These are the major revelations from the village regarding occupational diversification and its impact on education.

The development of non-caste occupations has taken place with the advent of small scale and cottage industries in this as well as the neighbouring villages. It has a pattern and exhibits the process of occupational diversification. Timber industries and tile factories are providing non-caste as well as non-traditional occupations within the village for the first time.

The socio-cultural conditions prevailing in our subcontinent have made obvious impact on every village, and it is reflected in the occupational status of the people.

Many members have adopted and/or achieved modern occupations in both government and private sectors. The study shows that the people of this village have obtained various new jobs not only due to the changes in the village life but also due to sudden changes in the occupational structure of our country. The inter-caste, inter-village, village-town, and national and international relations of the people, coupled with the communication network have been strengthened recently.

The studies on the inter-caste interactions of castes and communities (Lewis 1958, Mayer 1960, Srinivas 1962, Epstein 1962, Ishwaran 1968, Sarkar 1971, Misra 1988, Mann 1972, Varma 1977, Komoguchi 1984, Ekka 1985) explain various aspects of changes in the Indian villages of the yester years and the changes appeared recently. When the pattern of traditional occupations changed, it influenced the traditional interaction pattern of the villagers. The present interaction pattern is not based on the traditional services and jobs. The occupational diversification is the basic factor that paved the way for the change in the interaction pattern of the castes in the village and the very factor has facilitated the overall development and change.

The change in the pattern of interaction is an after-effect of the change in the overall socio-cultural change. Therefore, this aspect is quite significant. Occupational diversification and occupational shift from the traditional to the modern occupations are the causative factors for the present pattern of change in the inter-caste and inter-community proximal behaviours.

The pattern of social interaction of the people of the village is portrayed with the interpretations of Radcliffe-Brown; nevertheless, this elucidation does not fully depict the particular pattern of socio-cultural change of the heterogeneous population of the village.

As far as the caste and community interaction of this village is concerned, present data show that, earlier, almost all services and occupations were provided exclusively through the caste lines. The model or pattern of traditional caste interaction is referred to as Early Model-"*The Relations based on More Traditional Occupations and Less Modern Occupations*" and the Second Model, namely, the Contemporary Model, which is based on the "*The traditional and the modern occupational relations of the people of the village*".

It is important to note that, at present, only one-fourth of the households perpetuate their traditional occupation in the traditional manner, whereas three-fourth of the households have abandoned their traditional occupations and services. These figures point out the magnitude of change occurred within a village and it has in turn altered the very traditional mode of social interaction and led to the contemporary social structure.

Indian societies are organised on the basis of caste, and the network of this actually existing relations can be depicted as the social structure empirically. Any change in the elements of the nexus would reflect on the whole society. In India the caste groups and the members of castes are the elements and units in the traditional social structure.

The structural functional theory of Radcliffe-Brown and the structural theory of Levi-Strauss were helpful in providing a theoretical interpretation to the general principle of social interaction. However, these concepts and theories are inadequate to provide a clear picture of the socio-cultural change that is taking place in the multi-caste villages.

The present analysis reveals that there is a shift of emphasis in the concept of the people from 'dignity of occupation' to 'monetary benefit'. It means that the 'degree of dignity' of an occupation is measured not on the basis of the 'purity of occupation' but based on the income generated by an occupation. This is the one and the only reason for the occupational mobility towards goldwork in the village. At present, occupational mobility is taking place within the caste and outside the caste system. Again, the occupational mobility within the caste has two directions such as the upward and downward mobility. The upward mobility is rather common, whereas the downward mobility is rare. The occupational mobility is taking place only due to monetary concern. In this new situation, the applicability of the concept of Sanskritization becomes impossible. Moreover, Sanskritization does not mention anything about occupational change and its pattern.

The two-way process of occupational mobility, i.e., outside the caste system and within the caste system, are the two major directions discernible in the village communities in Kerala. The former development is mainly due to modern education, science and technology and the new occupational opportunities developed accordingly. The occupational mobility within the caste system is an alternative economic opportunity developed due to the inadequate growth of modern economy in the rural areas.

Occupational rigidity is non-existent today. Moreover, at present, there are no restrictions in selecting and relinquishing occupations; consequently many caste groups have adopted occupations of other castes. The Ezhavas adopted carpentry, masonry, goldwork, etc.; and the Nayars, Asari, Karuvan, Perumannan, Musari, etc., adopted goldwork. In general, almost all castes have adopted new or caste-free occupations, whereas other members have adopted the traditional caste occupations of other castes. In the context of urbanisation and modernisation, the former pattern of the adoption of occupation is common throughout India. But, the latter is very peculiar to a few caste groups, which have adopted the traditional occupation of other castes. This is the instance of occupational mobility within the caste occupations.

Economic aspect of the traditional occupations is also important because people continue their occupations in order to meet their livelihood. In general, people have abandoned their traditional occupations due to two major reasons, viz.: (1), due to less monetary gains; and (2), due to inferior social status. This type of occupational shift has been identified in the contiguous villages and other parts of Thrissur district in Kerala. The economic aspect has greater significance as the people are doing all services and jobs to meet their basic requirements of livelihood. Once the economic side of the occupations becomes weak, people move onto other areas of occupations for higher wages leading a better life.

At present, economic efficiency is the main basis for power and prestige in the village and not the prestige of occupations. *This shift of the old concept of occupations* (earlier occupations were considered high based on the purity of occupation) *to new occupation provides a pattern and it is referred to as Pecuniarisation.* Downward and upward occupational mobility pertaining to a particular occupation is the basic character of this phenomenon and this process is taking place all over Kerala. The concept of Pecuniarisation includes the same motivation and the two-way process of occupational mobility where the adoption of the traditional occupation of a caste by any other caste either as an individual or as a group merely with an economic motive is defined as Pecuniarisation.

When delineating the features of caste system Ghurye (1932; 1988 rpt.) pointed out that the traditional occupation is one among the characteristic features of the caste system. But, from the empirical evidence, today the traditional caste-based occupations are disappearing.

Although, a few people are perpetuating the caste-wise traditional occupations, most of the new generation are not interested to continue such occupations.

The Indian village is not as isolated entity although it can be regarded as one for empirical investigation (Varma 1977:15). Therefore, it is hoped that the theoretical explanations provided in this thesis would be useful for further research and analysis. This microcosmic study reveals that the shift from traditional occupation to new occupations is an underscorable change, and the occupational diversification and occupational mobility are making significant socio-cultural change in the village life. Many new cultural traits are added to the traditional life style, and many traits are being eradicated from the traditional life style.

The present day occupational diversification and occupational mobility are temporary arrangements for finding out livelihood, and this alone would not be enough to alter the caste system, though it indeed has resulted in the devastation and/or decline of the traditional occupation of a number of caste groups. Occupational diversification and occupational mobility are likely to continue in different directions according to the needs of the people and according to the growth of the population. Changes in occupation and services have however not affected the caste system as such.

Although, the occupations as well as the interaction pattern of the people have changed considerably, they continue to follow endogamous marriages and other religious aspects without much change. Economic sufficiency due to occupational diversification and occupational shift has prompted the villagers to form nuclear families, to conduct marriages without much financial burden, to impart good education to the new generation. In short, it also helped to enhance the general living standards.

Only a few categories of occupations existed in the village earlier. But with occupational diversification, more people have received better occupations for their livelihood, which have helped them to ameliorate their living condition greatly. Therefore, it is a fact that occupational diversification is a positive factor for the development of society by providing new and better job opportunities than the traditional occupations to the villagers. The occupational diversification has utmost importance and role in the present socio-cultural change, having provided better means of livelihood, earnings, and social status. My finding is that occupational diversification is the main factor for the present developments in the village. Occupational diversification has occurred within and outside the caste, as also within the village and outside. Diversification of occupations is also need-based. Among caste occupations, occupational mobility has occurred only with the aim of monetary benefit. Some of the caste occupations have disappeared only because they were less income-generating. Downward and upward occupational mobility are taking place within the caste occupations and it has a pattern. The concept of Sanskritization is not pertinent to explain this particular pattern. Therefore, Pecuniarisation, a new theory has been put forward here to explain the particular pattern of social and cultural change taking place among the unique as well as heterogeneous population of India.

GLOSSARY

Anthropology

Anthropology is a scientific study of man from social cultural point of view and biological view. Social anthropology is the study of social behaviour, especially from the point of the systematic comparative study of social forms and institution. Cultural anthropology is the study of the behaviours of man which are learned, including among others the social, linguistic, technical, and familial. Cultural anthropology has been called the study of man and his works.

Carrying capacity

Carrying capacity is the upper limit of the size of a population that a specific environment can support.

Caste

Caste is a social grouping into which a person is born and remains throughout his or her lifetime.

Caste Fission

During the course of history caste groups have divided into several subcastes due to various reasons. This split or fission of caste into subcastes is referred to as caste fission.

Caste Fusion

It is a concept that related to the fusion or blending of one or more subcastes and after fusion they will be known in a single name instead of respective subcaste name.

Caste Hierarchy

In the caste hierarchy the superior caste occupies the upper end of the hierarchy whereas lower castes positioned at the lower part of the latent hierarchical order of the society. Ritual purity and pollution is one of the factors for the hierarchical order of castes.

Consumer Culture

This is a popular concept that people buy every thing from market and they do not produce. It is argued that the consumer culture of the people spoils the small and unorganised producers of various edible and other items.

Culture

In anthropology the concept of culture is very broad. The way of life of people can be referred to as culture. Laymen view of culture normally connected to some specific art forms or paintings or literary work. In cultural anthropology, as has been established by E.B. Tylor, culture or civilisation taken in its wide ethnographic sense, is that complex whole which includes knowledge, belief, art, morals, law, custom, and any other capabilities and habits acquired by man as a member of society.

Diachronic

Referring to the historical or developmental approach to the study of culture. Diachronic studies take into account the dimension of time. Synchronic is the opposite view of diachronic. Synchronic referring to the functional approach to the study of culture, as of a given time.

Eco-cultural

The term 'eco-cultural' refers to the ecological and cultural interplay, which is an important perspective of the branch ecological anthropology.

Emic

Emic is a view of construal wherein the explication and presentation of indigenous models of reality. Etic is the opposite view of emic. The distinction between emics and etics in anthropology became popular for a time, used for the contrast between the explication and presentation of indigenous models of reality on the one hand and the description and comparison of sociocultural systems according to the observer's criteria on the other.

Endogamy

Endogamy is the rule of marriage between two people of the same social group or category. Endogamy is one of the features of caste system.

Ethnography

It is a category of anthropological research and it is characterised by the first-hand study of a small community or ethnic group. Such studies combine to a varying degree descriptive and analytical element. But the central characteristic of conventional ethnographies is that they focus on one specific culture or society and consider theoretical or comparative generalisations from the standpoint of the ethnographic example.

Exogamy

Marriage between people of different social groups and categories. The practice of a person seeking a mate outside his group usually found in clans and moieties. The terms exogamy and endogamy were coined by John F.Mc Lennan (1827-1881).

Monogamy

Monogamy is the most common form of marriage in which an individual has a single wife at any given time.

Genealogical Method

This technique of anthropology involves collecting and compiling pedigrees into tables of genealogy in order to determine kinship systems and the nature of the institutions. The technique was developed by W.H.R. Rivers while on the Torres Straits Expedition in 1898.

Socio-cultural Anthropology

The dominant tradition in British anthropology has generally been called 'social anthropology'. In modern anthropology in USA the term social anthropology is sometimes reserved to indicate the comparative study of societies and cultures, as opposed to the broader field of Cultural anthropology. In India, socio-cultural anthropology is a composite of both British and American perspective of anthropology.

Subcastes

The divisions of caste is known as subcastes. In many cases subcastes are also endogamous.

Synchronic

Synchronic studies analyses or theoretical approaches may be said to be Synchronic when they are characterised by the examination of data at a single moment in time or without regard for diachronic or historical process. The functional approach to the study of culture of a given time is also referred to as synchronic studies.

BIBLIOGRAPHY

AGRAWAL S.P. & AGGARWAL J.C. 1991. *Educational and Social Uplift of Backward Classes: At What cost and How? Mandal Commission and After*. New Delhi: Concept Publishing Company.

AINAPUR, L.S. 1986. *The Dynamics of Caste Relations in Rural India*. Jaipur: Rawat Publications.

AIYAPPAN, A. 1965. *The Personality of Kerala*. Trivandrum: Dept. of Publications, University of Kerala.

AIYAPPAN, A. 1965. *Social Revolution in a Kerala Village*. Bombay: Asia Publishing House.

AIYAPPAN A. & MAHADEVAN K. 1988. *Population and Social Change in an Indian village: Quarter Century of Development in Managadu Village, Tamil Nadu*. Delhi: Mittal Publications.

ALEXANDER K.C. 1975. Nature and Background of the Agrarian Unrest in Kuttanad, Kerala. *Journal of Kerala Studies*. Trivandrum; The Department of History, University of Kerala.

ALEXANDER, K.C. 1992. "Emergence of Agrarian Movements and class Consciousness Among south-Indian Peasantry" in *Rural Social Tranoformation*. Edited by S.K. Lal and U.R. Nahar. New Delhi: Rawat Publications.

ANANTHA KRISHNA IYER, L.K. 1987. *Landmarks in Indian Anthropology: Tribes and Castes of Cochin*. Vol. 15 (in 3 Parts) New Delhi: Cosmo Publication.

ANANTHA KRISHNA IYER, L.K. 1909. 1981 rpt. *The Tribes and Castes of Cochin*. Vol. II & III. New Delhi: Cosmo Publication.

ANANTHA KRISHNA IYER, L.K. 1939. (1981 rpt.). *The Travancore Tribes and Castes*. Vol. II & III New Delhi: Cosmo Publication.

ANSARI, A.W. 1980. *The Changing Village India*. New Delhi: Chetana Publications.

ANSARI, V. GOPALAKRISHNAN 1985. *Technological change for Rural Development in India*. Delhi: B.R. Publishing Corporation.

ATAL, YOGESH 1968. (1979 rpt.) *Changing Frontiers of Caste*. New Delhi: National Publishing House.

ATAL, YOGESH 1976. *Social Sciences, The Indian Scene*. New Delhi; Abhinav Publications.

BADEN-POWELL, B.H. 1899. (1986 rpt.). *The Origin and Growth of Village Communities in India*. New Delhi: University Book Service.

BASANT, RAKESH 1994. "Economic Diversification in Rural Areas: Review of Process with Special Reference to Gujarat" in *Economic and Political Weekly*. Vol. XXXIX No. 39 September. Bombay: A Sameeksha Trust Publication.

BETEILLE, ANDRE 1965. (1971 rpt). *Caste, Class and Power*. London: University of California Press.

BETEILLE, ANDRE 1972. *Inequality and Social Change*. Delhi: Oxford University Press.

BETEILLE, ANDRE 1974. *Six Essays in Comparative Sociology*. Delhi: Oxford University Press.

BHANU, B. ANANDA & MAHENDRAKUMAR, M.S. 2000. *Kottakkal Village, Malappuram District. Village India Project*. New Delhi: IGNCA & UNESCO *(unpublished)*.

BHARADWAJ, A.N. 1979. *The Problems of SCs & STs in Kerala*. New Delhi: Light & Life Publication.

BHASKARANUNNI, P. 1988. *Patthonpatham Noottandile Keralam* (study in Malayalam), Trichur: Kerala Sahitya Akademi.

BHENDE, ASHA A. & KANITKAR, TARA 1996. *Principles of Population Studies*. Bombay: Himalaya Publishing House.

BOSE, NIRMAL KUMAR 1975 rpt. "Some Aspects of Caste in Bengal" in *Traditional India: Structure and Change*. Edited by Milton Singer. Jaipur: Rawat Publications.

BOHANNAN, PAUL & GLAZER, MARK 1973. *High Points in Anthropology*. New York: Alfred A. Knopf.

Census 1931. Simla: Office of the Census Commissioner for India.

Census 1961. Simla: Office of the Census Commissioner for India.

CHAKRABORTI, S.B. 1983. "Management of Land and Labour in a West Bengal Village: Some Observations" in *Human Science*, Vol.32, No. 4. Calcutta: Anthropological Survey of India.

CHAKRABORTI, S.B., GHOSH B.R. & AJIT K. DANDA 1985. *Agrarian Situation in India*. Vol. I & II. Calcutta: Anthropological Survey of India.

CHAUHAN, BRIJ RAJ 1974. "Rural Studies, a Trend Report" in *A Survey of Research in Sociology and Social Anthropology*. Vol. 1, Bombay: Popular Prakashan.

JOHN, BERNARD S. 1975 rpt. "Changing Traditions of a Low Caste" in *Traditional India: Structure and Change*. Edited by Milton Singer. Jaipur: Rawat Publications.

DANDA, AJIT K. 1986. "Development Perspective and the Rural Poor". in *Human Science* Vol. 35. No.3. Calcutta: Anthropological Survey of India.

DANDA, AJIT K. 1986. "Forms and Nature of Stratification in a West Bengal Village" in *Human Science*. Vol. 35, No. 1. Calcutta: Anthropological survey of India.

DAK, T.M. 1982. *Social Inequalities and Rural Development*. New Delhi: National Publishing House.

DEOGAONKAR, S.G. 1980. *Administration for Rural Development in India*. New Delhi: Concept Publishing Company.

DESAI, A.R. 1979. *Rural India in Transition*. Bombay: Popular Prakashan.

DESAI, A.R. (Ed.) 1986. *Agrarian Struggles in India after Independence*. Delhi: Oxford University Press.

DIWAN, PARAS & DIWAN PEEYUSHI 1972. (1995 rpt.) *Modern Hindu Law*. Allahabad: Allahabad Law Agency.

DUBE, S.C. 1955. (1965 rpt.) *Indian Village*. London: Routledge and Kegan Paul Ltd.

DUTTA, SUJIT KUMAR 1987. "Social Relations of Production in Bihar's Villages: An Experimental Exploration" in *Human Science*. Vol. 36. No. 4. Calcutta: Anthropological Survey of India.

EKKA, WILLIAM 1985. "Caste Hierarchy and Inter-ethnic relationship in a Village of Surguja Dt. Madhya Pradesh" in *Human science* Vol.34. No. 3. Calcutta: Anthropological Survey of India.

EMBER, CAROL R. & EMBER, MELVIN 1973. (1985 rpt). *Cultural Anthropology*. New Jersey: Prentice Hall, Inc.

EPSTEIN, T.S. 1962. *Economic Development and Social Change in South India*. Manchester: Manchester University Press.

FAWCETT, F. 1901. (1990 rpt.) *Nayars of Malabar*. New Delhi: Asian Educational Services.

FRANCIS DAY, 1863. (1990 rpt). *The Land of the Perumals of Cochin its Past and its Present*. New Delhi: Asian Educational Service.

FREEMAN, J.A. 1974. "Occupational Changes in Urbanising Hindu Village" in *Man In India*, Vol. 54, No. 1.

FULLER, C.J. 1976. *The Nayars Today*. London: Cambridge University Press.

FULLER, C.J. (Ed.) 1996. *Caste Today*. Bombay: Oxford University Press.

GHURYE, G.S. 1935. (1942 & 1986 rpt.), *Caste and Race in India*. Bombay: Popular Prakashan.

GHURYE, G.S. 1963. *The Anatomy of a Rural-Urban Community*. Bombay: Popular Prakashan.

GOUGH, E. KATHLEEN & SCHNEIDER, DAVID M. (Eds) 1961. *Matrilineal Kinship*. Berkely: University of California Press.

GOUGH, E. KATHLEEN (1975 rpt.), "Cults of the Dead Among the Nayars" in *Traditional India: Structure and Change*. Edited by Milton singer. Jaipur: Rawat Publications.

GOULD, HAROLD A. 1988. *Caste Adaptation in Modernizing Indian Society*. Delhi: Chanakya Publications.

GUPTA, ARABINDA DATTA 1978. "Occupational Mobility among some castes in Ponnampet, A Coorg Village" in *Bulletin*, Vol. XXVII, Nos. 1 & 2. (January-June) Calcutta: Anthro-pological Survey of India.

GUPTA, BIMAN KUMAR DAS 1981. "Village Council and Inter-village Solidarity Among the Purum Chote of Manipur" in *Bulletin* Vol. XXIV, Nos. 1 & 2. Calcutta: Anthropological Survey of India.

GUPTA, PRANAB KUMAR DAS 1985. "The Scale of Industriali-sation and Differential Cultural Adaptation". in *Human Science* Vol. 34, No. 2, Calcutta: Anthropological Survey of India.

GURUMURTHY, K.G. 1988. *Rural Development and Factional Politics*. New Delhi: Reliance Publishing House.

HARRIS, MARVIN 1983. *Cultural Anthropology*. (Ed-2). New York: Harper & Row Publishers.

HARDESTRY, DONALD L. 1977. *Ecological Anthropology*. New York: John Wiley & Sons.

HASNAIN, NADEEM 1991. *Indian Anthropology*. Delhi: Palaka Prakashan.

HIRAMANI, A.B. 1977. *Social Change in Rural India: A Study of Two Villages in Maharashtra*. Delhi: B.R. Publishing Corporation.

HUTTON, J.H. 1946. (1986 rpt.), *Caste in India: Its Nature, Function, and Origins*. Delhi: Oxford University Press.

ISHWARAN, K. 1968. *Shivapur: A South Indian Village*. London: Routledge & Kegan Paul.

JEFFREY, ROBIN 1976. *The Decline of Nayar Dominance*. London: Sussex University Press.

JHA, HETUKAR, 1991. *Social Structures of Indian Villages: A study of Rural Bihar*. New Delhi: Sage Publications.

JHA, MAKHAN 1994. *An Introduction to Social Anthropology*. New Delhi: Vikas Publishing House Pvt. Ltd.

JODHKA, SURINDER S. 1994. "Agrarian Changes and Attached Labour Emerging Patterns in Haryana Agriculture" in *Economic and Political Weekly*; Vol. XXIX No. 39. (September). Bombay: A Sameeksha Trust Publication.

KAMESWARA RAO, N.V. 1979. "Saga of Development in a Telungana Village" in *Bulletin* Vol. XXIII. Nos. 1 & 2. Calcutta: Anthropological Survey of India.

KARASHIMA, NOBORA (Ed.) 1983. *Socio-cultural change in Villages in Tiruchirapalli Dt. Tamil Nadu, India*. Part-I Pre-Modern Period. Tokyo: Institute for the Study of Languages and cultures of Asia and Africa.

Kerala District Gazetteers 1981. *Trichur Supplement*. Trivandrum: Kerala Gazetteers Department.

KEESING, ROGER, M. 1981. *Cultural Anthropology: A Contemporary Perspective*. New York: Holt, Rinehart and Winston.

KOMOGUCHI, YOSHIMI 1984. "A South Indian Village: Its Agriculture and Community" in *Socio-cultural change in Villages in Tiruchirapalli Dt. In Tamil Nadu*, Part-II Modern Period No. 3. Tokyo: Institute for the study of Languages and cultures of Asia and Africa (ILCAA), Tokyo University of Foreign Studies.

KRISHNAN EZHUTHACHAN, V.R. 1997. *V.R. Krishnan Ezhuthachan –Atmakatha* (Autobiography). Thrissur: Published by the author.

KRISHNA IYER, L.A. 1961. *Kerala and Her People*. (Name of Publisher not available)

KUNDU, N.N. 1978. "Landowner-Tenant Relationship in a Maharastra Village" in *Bulletin*; Vol. XXVII, Nos. 1 & 2 Calcutta: Anthropological Survey of India.

KURIAN, V. MATHEW 1986. *The Caste-Class Formations: A Case Study of Kerala*. New Delhi: B.R. Publishing Corporation.

KURUP, K.K.N. 1982. *Modern Kerala: Research Papers in History*. Trivandrum: State Institute of Languages.

KURUP, K.K.N. 1988. *Modern Kerala* (Studies in Social and Agrarian Relations) Delhi: Mittal Publications.

LAKSHMINARAYANA, H.D. 1976. *India's Villages at Cross-roads*. New Delhi: National Publishing House.

LEMERCINIER, GENEVIEVE 1974. (1994 rpt.). *Religion and Ideology in Kerala*. (First published in Belgium by Centre Tricontinental Louvain-la-Neuve) Trivandrum: Institute for the Study of Developing Areas.

LEVI-STRAUSS, CLAUDE 1963. (1986 rpt.) *Structural Anthropology*. England (UK) : Penguin Books.

LEWIS, OSCAR 1954. *Group Dynamics in North Indian Village*. Delhi: Planning Commission.

LEWIS, OSCAR 1958. *Village Life in Northern India*. Urbana: University of Illinois Press.

LIETEN, GEORGE KRISTOFFEL 1975. "The Economic Structure of Kerala in the Mid-Fifties" in *Journal of Kerala Studies*. Vol. II Part IV, Kerala: Department of History, Kerala University.

MADAN, G.R. 1979. *India's Social Transformation, Vol. Problems of Economic Development*. New Delhi: Allied Publishers Pvt. Ltd.

MADAN, G.R. & DASGUPTA, SATADAL 1968. *Bulletin* Vol. XVII, No. I. Calcutta: Anthropological Survey of India.

MAJUMDAR, D.N. 1958. *Caste and Communication in an Indian Village*. New Delhi: Asia Publishing House.

MALAVIYA, H.D. 1987 rpt. "Village Communities In India: A Historical Outline" In *Rural Sociology In India*. Edited by A.R. Desai. Bombay: Popular Prakashan.

MANDAL, S.K. & BHAKRABARTH, KAKALI 1991. "Agro-economic Organisation Among The Jats: A Study In A South Rajastan Village". In *Journal of The Anthropological Survey of India*. Vol. 40, No. 1 & 2.

MANDELBAUM, DAVID G. 1970. *Society in India*. Bombay: Popular Prakashan.

MANICKAVASAGAM 1990. "Brahmins" in *Dravidian Encyclopaedia*. Edited by V.I. Subramoniam. Trivandrum: International School of Dravidian Linguistics.

MANN, R.S. 1972. "Social Stratification and Interaction in Ladakhi Villages" in *Bulletin* Vol. XXI, No. 3 & 4. Calcutta: Anthropological Survey of India.

MANN, R.S. 1984. *Anthropological and Sociological Theory: Approaches And Applications*. Jaipur: Rawat Publications.

MANN, R.S. 1987. *Social Change and Social Research (An Indian Perspective)* New Delhi: Concept Publishing Company.

MAMMEN P. MAMMEN 1975. "Traditional Kerala Society". In *Journal of Kerala Studies*, Vol. II Part III. Trivandrum: Dept. of History, University of Kerala.

MAYER, ADRIAN C. 1960. (1986 rpt.) *Caste And Kinship in Central India: A Village and Its Region*. New Delhi: Universal Book Stall.

MATHUR, P.R.G. 1977. "Socio-economic Changes Among The Weaker Sections of The Population of Kerala". In *Journal of Kerala Studies* Vol. IV March 1977, Part-I. Trivandrum: Dept. of History, University of Kerala.

MENON, C. ACHYUTA 1911. (1995 rpt.) *The Cochin State Manual*. Thiruvananthapuram: Kerala Gazetteers Department.

MENON, KOMATTIL ACHYUTHA 1961. *Ancient Kerala: Studies in its History and Culture*. Trichur: Kumari T.C. Jayashree.

MENON, A. SREEDHARA 1979. *Social and Cultural History of India: Kerala*. New Delhi: Sterling Publishers Pvt. Ltd.

MILLER ROLAND, E. 1976. *Mappila Muslims of Kerala: A Study in Islamic Trends*. New Delhi: Orient Longman.

MISRA, BIDYADHAR 1988. *Village Life in India: Past and Present*. Delhi: Ajanta Publications.

MISRA, RAJALAKSHMI 1979. "Spatial and Socio-economic Gaps Between Harijan and the Other Castes in Tamil Nadu Villages". *Bulletin* Vol. XXIII, Nos. 1 & 2 Calcutta: Anthropological Survey of India.

MOHANACHANDRAN, S. 1993. "Velanmarude Jeevithavum Samskaravum" in *Samskarakeralam* (Quarterly in Malayalam) Vol. 7, No. 3. Kerala; Department of Cultural Publications.

MOORE, WILBERT, E. 1974. (1994 rpt.) *Social Change*. New Delhi: Prentice-hall of India Pvt. Ltd.

MORAB, S.G., SURESH PATIL & B.R. GHOSH, 1985. "Agrarian Situation in Karnataka: Some Observations From a Village In Chitradurga District" in *Human Science*: Vol. 34, No. 4. December 1985. Calcutta: Anthropological Survey of India.

MUKHOPADHYAY, K. 1989. "Democratisation of Village Panchayat: A Study of a Karnataka Village" in *Human Science* Vol. 38. No. 1. Calcutta: Anthropological Survey of India.

MURDOCK, GEORGE PETER 1949. (1965 rpt.), *Social Structure*. New York: The Free Press.

MUTHUMANI, M.K. 2000. *Social and Cultural Anthropology*. New Delhi: Commonwealth Publishers.

NAKAMURA, HISASHI 1982. "Disintegration and Re-integration of Rural Society in the Process of Economic Development: The Second Survey of a Tank-based Village in Tamil Nadu" in *Studies in Socio-cultural Change in Rural Villages in Tiruchirapalli District, Tamil Nadu, India*. No. 5. Tokyo; Institute for the Study of Languages and Cultures of Asia and Africa.

NAMBOODIRIPAD, E.M.S. 1994. *The Communist Party in Kerala: Six Decades of Struggle and advance*. New Delhi: National Book Centre.

NAMBOODIRIPAD, E.M.S. 1995. "Kerala Charithravum Jativyavastayum" In *Samskarakeralam* (A Malayalam Quarterly) April-june 1995. Kerala: Department Of Cultural Publications.

National Classification of Occupations (Nco) 1958. Govt. of India: Directorate General of Employment and Training (Occupational Information Unit), Ministry of Labour, Employment and Rehabilitation.

OOMMEN, M.A. 1979. "Land Reforms and Agrarian Change in Kerala Since Independence" in *Kerala Economy Since Independence* Edited by M.A. Oommen. New Delhi: Oxford & IBH Publishing Co.

OPLER, MORRIS & R.B. SINGH 1948. "The Division of Labour in an Indian Village" in *A Reader in General Anthropology* Edited by C.S. Coon. (464-496).

OPLER, MORRIS 1951. *Village Life in North India*. Chicago: The Delphian Society.

OSELLA, FILIPPO & OSELLA, CAROLINE 2000. *Social Mobility in Kerala–Modernity and Identity in Conflict*. London: Pluto Press.

OSWALT, WENDELL H. 1986. *Life Cycles and Lifeways: An Introduction to Cultural Anthropology*. Palo Alto, California: Mayfield Publishing Company.

PADMANABHA MENON, K.P. 1983. *History of Kerala*, Vol. II, New Delhi; Asian Educational Service.

PILLAI, A.K.B. 1987. *The Culture of Social Stratification / Sexism, The Nayars*. Massachusetts: Copley Publishing Group.

POORNIMA VARMA 1977. *Social Organisaation of Amnari: A Village Study in Chotanagpur*. Calcutta: Institute of Social Research & Applied Anthropology.

POTHAN, S.G. 1963. *The Syrian Christians of Kerala*. New Delhi: Asia Publishing House.

PRAMODKUMAR & KANTH, B.N. 1995. "Employment Prospects of Cottage and Small Scale Industries: A Case Study of Mahe", in *Southern Economist*, May-15, 1995.

RADCLIFFE-BROWN, A.R. 1976. *Structure and Function in Primitive Society*. London: Routledge & Kegan Paul.

RADHAKRISHNAN, P. 1989. *Peasant Struggles, Land Reforms and Social Change, Malabar 1836–1982*. New Delhi: Sage Publications.

RAO, D. VASUDEVA 1985. *Facets of Rural Development in India*. New Delhi: Ashish Publishing House.

RAO, M.S.A. 1972. *Tradition, Rationality and Change*. Bombay: Popular Prakashan.

RAO, SANGEETHA R. 1989. *Caste System in India: Myth and Reality*. New Delhi: India Publishers and Distributors.

RAO, SHANKAR C.N. 1994. *Sociology*. New Delhi: S. Chand & Company Ltd.

RIZVI, B.R. 1979. "Social Stratification in Western Himalayas; A Comparative Study of the Bodhs of Spiti and Muslims of Kargil" in *Bulletin* Vol. XXIII, (1974 January–June) No. 1 & 2, Calcutta: Anthropological Survey of India.

ROY BURMAN, B.K. 1984. "Changing Agrarian Relations and Ethnic Process in a Cluster of Villages in West Bengal" in *Human Science*. Vol. 33, No. 3, Calcutta: Anthropological Survey of India.

SANKARAN NAMBOODIRIPADU, KANIPAYYUR 1962. *Nayanmarude Poorva Charithram (History of Nayars)* Part I & II. Kunnamkulam, Kerala: Panchangam Pustakasala.

SARKAR, JAYANTA 1984. *Caste, Occupation and Change*. Delhi: B.R. Publishing Corporation.

SCHNEIDER, DAVID, M. & KATHLEEN GOUGH (eds.) 1961. (1974 rpt) *Matrilineal Kinship*. California: University of California Press.

SCUPIN, RAYMOND 1995. *Cultural Anthropology a Global Perspective*. New Jersey: Prentice Hall.

SHARMA, DAVENDRA K. & SULBHA JOSHI 1981. *Planning for the Poor*. Bhopal: Institute of Regional Analysis.

SHARMA, H.R. 1994. "Distribution of Landholdings in Rural India, 1953-54 to 1981-82: Implications for Land Reforms" in *Economic and Political Weekly*. Vol. XXIX No. 39, September. Bombay: A Sameeksha Trust Publication.

SINHA, ANAND KUMAR & LAL BABU SINGH 1992. "Occupational Mobility Among the Harijans of Urban Bihar" in *Man and Life* Vol. 18, Nos. 3 & 4. Calcutta: Institute of Social Research & Applied Anthropology.

SING, K.S. (ed.) 1998. *People of India–National Series Vol. IV, India's Communities*. Anthropological Survey of India, Kolkata. Delhi: Oxford University Press.

SINGER, MILTON 1975 rpt. "The Great Tradition in a Metropolitan Center: Madras" in *Traditional India: Structure and Change*. Edited by Milton Singer. Jaipur: Rawat Publications.

SINGH, YOGENDRA 1977. (1980 Rpt.), *Social Stratification and Change in India*. New Delhi: Manohar Book Service.

SINHA, ANIL KISHORE 1992. "Occupational Mobility in West Bengal with Special Reference to Moyra Caste" in *Man and Life*. Vol.18. Nos. 1 & 2, Calcutta: Institute of Social Research & Applied Anthropology.

SIVARAM, P. 1990. *Social Mobility: A Sociological Study*. New Delhi: Discovery Publishing House.

SRINIVAS, M.N. 1942. *Marriage and Family in Mysore*. Man; Vol.46. No. 86.

SRINIVAS, M.N. 1952. *Religion and Society Among the Coorgs of South India*. Delhi: Oxford University Press.

SRINIVAS, M.N. 1955. "Social Structure of a Mysore Village" in *Village India*. Edited by Mckim Marriot. Chicago: University of Chicago.

SRINIVAS, M.N. 1960. *India's Villages*. (2 edn). Bombay: Asia Publishing House.

SRINIVAS, M.N. 1976. (1979 rpt.) *The Remembered Village*. Delhi: Oxford University Press.

SRINIVAS, M.N. et al. 1977. *Dimensions of Social Change in India*. New Delhi: Allied Publishers Pvt. Ltd.

SRINIVAS, M.N. 1962. (1977 rpt.) *Caste in Modern India and Other Essays*. Bombay: Asia Publishing House.

SRINIVAS, M.N. 1966. (1995 rpt.) *Social Change in Modern India*. New Delhi: Orient Longman Ltd.

SHARMA, MADAN LAL & DAK, T.M. 1985. *Caste and Class in Agrarian Society: Dynamics of Rural Development.* Delhi: Ajanta Publications.

SUBBIAH, S. 1981. "Rural Base in A South Indian Village: A Study Into Its Structural and Spatial Patterns in Mahizambadi Village of Tamil Nadu" in *Studies in Socio-cultural Change in Rural Villages in Tiruchirapalli District, Tamil Nadu, India.* No. 4. Tokyo: Institute for the Study of Languages and Cultures of Asia and Africa.

SUKUMARAPILLA, K. 1994. "Nayarum Namboodiriyum" in *Samskarakeralam* (Quarterly in Malayalam) Vol. 8, No. 1. Kerala: Department of Cultural Publications.

THAKUR, B.N. 1988. *Sociology of Rural Development*. New Delhi: Classical Publishing Company.

THURSTON, EDGAR 1909. (1975 rpt.), *Castes and Tribes of Southern India*. Vol. I to VII (Madras: Govt. Press), Delhi: Cosmo Publications.

TSUKASA MIZUSHIMA & TSUYOSHI NARA 1981. "Social Change in a Dry Village in South India: an Interim Report" in *Studies in Socio-cultural Change in Rural Villages in Tirichirapalli District, Tamil Nadu, India.* No. 4. Tokyo: Institute for the Study of Languages and Cultures of Asia and Africa.

TURNER, JONATHAN & MARYANSKI, ALEXANDRA 1979. *Functionalism.* California: The Benjamin/Cumming Publishing Company.

TYLOR, EDWARD, B. 1871. *Primitive Culture–Researches into the Development of Mythology, Philosophy, Religion, Language, Art, And Custom.* London: John Murray, Albemarle Street.

UPADHYAY,V.S. & GAYA PANDEY 1993. (1997 rpt.). *History of Anthropological Thought*. New Delhi: Concept Publishing Company.

VARGHESE, N.V. 1999. "Access Versus Achievement—A Study of Primary Education in Kerala" in Rethinking Development Keralas Development Experience Vol. 2. Edited By M.A. Oommen. New Delhi: Concept Publishing Company.

VARMA, 1977. *Social Organisation of Amnari: A Village Study in Chotanagpur*. Calcutta: Institute of Social Research & Applied Anthropology.

VELAYUDHAN, P.S. 1979. *Social and Religious Movements in Kerala in the Nineteenth and Twentieth Centuries* Calcutta: Institute of Historical Studies.

VERGHESE, K.E. 1986. *Socio-economic Change in Kerala*. New Delhi: Ashish Publishing House.

VIDYARTHI, L.P. 1978. *Rise of Anthropology in India,* Vol. II. Delhi: Concept Publishers.

VIDYARTHI, L.P. (ed.) 1982. *Rural Development in South Asia*. New Delhi: Concept Publishing Company.

WARD & CONNER, LIEUTENANTS. 1863. (1994 rpt) *Memoir of the Survey of the Travancore and Cochin States* Vol. I & II. Thiruvananthapuram: Kerala Gazetteers Department.

WILLIAM LOGAN, M.C.S. 1981 rpt. *Malabar Manual*. Trivandrum: Charithram Publications.

WISER, W.H. 1936. *Hindu Jajmani System*. Lucknow: Asia Publishing House.

YOUNG, PAULINE V. 1966. (1992 rpt.) *Scientific Social Surveys and Research*. New Delhi: Prentice-hall of India Pvt. Ltd.

INDEX

Acculturation 140, 152
Agriculture 135-138
Ayurveda 65, 87, 133
Brahmanisation 8
Caste 13
Caste fission 184
Caste fusion 69, 184
Caste, endogamous 3, 13
Caste tag 142-143
Commensal contacts 14
Commensal hierarchy 13-14
Commensal status 14
Consumer culture 113, 152
Culture, definition 130-131
Culture area 175
Diachronic 5
Dominant caste 9, 107
Door to door selling 113, 114
Dowry 158, 191
Educational status 172
Endogamy 156
Environmental Determinism, ecology 137
Family 159, 160, 161
Family, definition 159, 160
Family, extended 166
Family, broken nuclear 168
Function 103
Function, Bohnan and Glazer 104
Function, Malinowski 105
Function, Malinowski 105
Function, Radcliffe-Brown 103
Genealogical structure 165
In-migration 169
Institute of Developing Economies, Japan 23
Inter Caste marriages 157
Kerala Agrarian Relations Act 186
Kerala Land Reforms Act 118-119, 186
Komazawa University, Japan 23
Kuttanand 33
Marxist and Communist Party 34, 35, 119
Marriage, definition 153-154
Master-slave relationship 117, 118

Mini-Industrial Estate 101
Monogamy 156
Nair Service Society (NSS) 185
Occupational diversification, definition 77, 101, 148, 154, 159, 171, 177, 187, 189, 190
Occupational mobility 2, 3, 29, 29, 30, 189
Occupational structure 72
Parallel Occupations 110-111
Pecuniarisation 2, 187
Pecuniarisation, definition 2, 186-187
Pecuniarisation, theory 2
People of India Project 74
Powell, Baden 78
Proximal distance 117-118
Proximal behaviours 126
Sadhu Jana Paripalana Yogam 184
Sanskritization 7, 8, 106, 181, 182, 183, 186
Siva Narayan sect 17
Sri Narayana Dharma Paripalana Yogam (SNDP) 184
Social structure 5, 104, 105, 127, 129
Social structure, Levi-Strauss 127
Social structure, Radcliffe-Brown 127
Structure 103, 105
Structural Functional theory, Radcliffe-Brown 129
Structural theory, Levi-Strauss 129
Structural model 127
Subcaste 13, 112
Synchronic 5
Thrissur 41-46, 138, 140
Twicw-Born Castes 108-109
University of Madras 22
University of Tokyo 23
University, Madhurai-Kamaraj 22
Village,
    Amaravila village 31
    Amnari village 18
    Anjumoorthy village 33
    Ankamali village 31
    Anthicad village 32
    Attapadi village 32
    Basudha village 26
    Bengal village 16
    Bharanikavu village 31
    Bhoupur village 24
    Bhuimohan village 24
    Champakad village 32
    Cheruvannur village 32
    Cherpu village 100
    Chetna village 24
    Chingeri village 32
    Chotanagpur village 18
    Coorg village 6
    Danela village 15
    Edakkad village 32
    Edamon village 31
    Eravipuram village 31
    Golatgaon village 18
    Hampapura village 28
    Hirearakere village 25
    Insura village 24
    Jajigram village 16
    Jamma village 24
    Kadakkavoor village 31

Kadapra village 31
Kadukkamkunnam village 32
Kerala villages 31, 37
Kolghar village 18
Kottakkal village 36
Kottukal village 31
Kumbapetti village 6
Kurichy village 32
Ladakhi village 16
Ladpur village 15
Lokamaleswaram village 32
Mahizambadi village 22
Malwa village 12
Manhalli village 6
Manikpur village 27
Mavli village 29
Mulavucad village 31
Muttar village 31
Muttil village 32
Naduvannur village 32
Namhalli village 6
Nemmara village 32
Nenmanukkara village 100
Nilambur village 32
Ollur village 100
Palayasivaram village 20
Palode village 32
Pampur village 15
Panancherry village 32
Parassala village 31
Periyar village 32
Piragram village 24
Prakkad village 31
Purum Chote village 22
Ramkheri village 12
Rampur village 12
Rampura village 6
Sardi village 25
Sargaria village 24
Shamirpet village10
Shankarpur village 27
Shivpur village 8
Sujanpur village 27
Telengana village 19
Thalikulam village 32
Thankasseri village 31
Thazhava village 31
Thekkumbhagam village 31
Thirunelly village 32
Thiruvangad village 32
Urakam village 100
Vallachira village 37, 43, 44,
Vinzar village 19
Wangala village 15

Westernisation 8, 181